D0514589

Unbrandable.

Un
brand
able.

#HowToSucceedIn
TheNewBrandSpace

#AdamNStone

Thames & Hudson

To Ali – my brand brother and oldest friend

The author and publisher gratefully acknowledge the permissions that have
been granted to reproduce copyright material in this book. While every effort
has been made to trace copyright holders and to obtain their permission for the
use of such material, the publisher will be happy to correct in subsequent
editions any errors or omissions that are brought to its attention.

Unbrandable: How to Succeed in the New Brand Space © 2015 Adam N. Stone

Designed by Steve Russell

First published in 2015 in paperback in the United States of America by
Thames & Hudson Inc., 500 Fifth Avenue, New York, New York 10110

thamesandhudsonusa.com

Library of Congress Catalog Card Number 2014952826

ISBN 978-0-500-29192-4

Printed and bound in China by Everbest Printing Co., Ltd

Contents

Introduction: It's All Changed – Again

There will always be the majority and the minority. In economic (and brand/advertising) terms, this means that there will always be a mass market for stuff that no one really needs. A solar-powered waving queen, the latest mobile phone, a more powerful car, the most advanced anti-ageing cosmetics, some retro-styled MC Hammer pants. This market is as manufactured as the products it consumes. To keep the system pumping, a hyper-reality is created (enter the advertising, entertainment and news/media industries) that generates a 'need' for the aforementioned products, one that is sustained by all means necessary: the cult of celebrity, sex, drugs, debt/credit, ego/one-upmanship, the psychological manufacture of desire. This is the shop window of the neoclassical economic regime, and – from some angles, at least – it's looking a bit tired, rather worn out.

The good news is that amid all this retail madness a paradigm shift is taking place. The voice of the minority (which used to be known as the 1 per cent, but now it's more like the 10 per cent), the voice of the unwavering, not-for-sale freedom-from-the-onslaught-of-brand-bullshit-fighters, is calling for a change. These are the Unbrandables, a growing number of people who have had enough of the propaganda (both political and commercial); of the neglect of the planet; of the relentless, reward-less, debt-driven rat race; of the (credit) cards being stacked against them by the people who actually run things; of the environment-damaging products they neither want nor need. Using the power of choice, which controls their wallet, they are demanding a new form of economics: a new model for living, working and buying. And because this means they have an economic impact, slowly but surely their voice is being heard. Perhaps one day it will be the majority that is Unbrandable, and all brands will act accordingly.

'We can abandon everything we thought we knew about progress. We completely re-imagine industry, nutrition, communication, transportation and housing. We rehabilitate consumer culture, and create a level and holistic playing field for living and future generations. Humanity, and the world it depends on, are sustained.'

Kalle Lasn, co-founder, Adbusters Media Foundation

This new economic philosophy requires a new language of advertising, a new method of brand communication that is honest, relevant, engaging, ecologically sound and, most importantly, enlightening. Above all, in order for any of this to be successful – in order for the brands to be able to engage with this new, Unbrandable audience – a new way of thinking is needed. This book is an exploration of some of the ideas, thoughts and concepts that could influence the new visual language and method of communication that we call 'content'. From portraits of interesting Unbrandable people doing fascinating things globally to case studies of successful Unbranded brands and examples of digital-media streams that actually work, this book is all about how to connect with the Unbrandables.

'I personally believe that the future of advertising needs to be about creating utility and smart tools – for people to care about your products and brand.'

Victoria Nyberg, strategist at Wednesday

Of the many eye-opening experiences I had while researching this book, one of the most surreal was watching an African refugee dressed as a traditional Chinese peasant (conical hat, comedy kung-fu suit) shuffling around Moscow's Red Square in front of the most exclusive shops in the city – Louis Vuitton, Chanel – while trying to hand out leaflets for something, an exhibition on the art of war, perhaps, or maybe a Thai buffet. Wasn't this meant to be some kind of shrine to Communism? Didn't this place used to be culturally important? But there I was, sandwiched between high-end shops and low-end flyering, and no one – apart from yours truly – was willing to suggest that something was amiss.

Fast forward by a few months and I'm in a meeting room of the Hurlingham Club in Fulham, south-west London, with the head of spirits for Diageo, the Smirnoff Africa brand manager and the bloke who invented the 99-cent iTunes download for Apple (who we'll hear from later), so heavy hitters on all sides. I tell them that I can't guarantee that the quite considerable budget they're thinking of giving me for a project will actually affect the amount of vodka sold, but that they (and their brand) will get a ton of good vibes from the project, which was to mentor and develop emerging talents from the African continent. No one bats an eyelid. They tell me not to worry about all that, that they just want to do some good, to spread the love. I nearly fall off my chair. I am so conditioned to having to fight to get good, honest, decent work past the client's beady eye. Isn't this all a bit left field? Where are all the men in suits, staring me down after I've presented my visions, tut-tutting and sighing before they go on to tell me that – regrettably – what I'm proposing to do is way too 'edgy', all a bit too 'niche'? I reckon that the times, they are a-changing.

In whatever sphere you operate, moving forwards means progressing from one idea to the next. And this is where the Unbrandables come in. With regards to the economic (and cultural) paradigm shift mentioned earlier, and the corresponding rise of the Unbrandables, mainstream, above-the-line advertising is the proverbial dead shark. It's annoying, irrelevant, archaic – and these are its good points. Often, a lot of it is created for other advertising executives, for the in-crowd. I recently reconnected with a copywriting legend who had just retired. He told me that he still met a lot of 'advertising wankers', but now he didn't have to listen to them. For whatever reason, mainstream advertising is no longer about creating content that people want to engage with, that says something to them about their lives. Which is what my last book, *The Stuff You Can't Bottle* (2013), is all about, albeit in relation to the youth market.

This book is the next step on a journey of discovery: a study ofhow the methods of brand communication have to change in line with the economic climate in order to stay in tune with the mindset of the Unbrandables, and of how buying, selling and all the good stuff in between has to mutate into something else. Something new. It's about how a growing number of people have – seemingly – lost all faith in brands, the consequence being that they try to block their eyes and ears to the constant spiel that bombards their every waking moment. The rebel in me loves the idea of this, but deep down I know that the onslaught of brands is unstoppable – but that shouldn't deter us from trying to fight the bad and celebrate the good. There are brands out there that understand the new brand space, and there are many more that will soon join them; there will always be others, however, that behave like the school bully and ride roughshod over the cultural landscape.

I spend a lot of time these days talking to clients about this new 'brand space', and even though I'm not sure how much actually gets through, there are quite a few of us preaching the new gospel. One important and culturally relevant point here is that as long as there are people reacting against what is happening in the world, something beautiful and original will be created, and it is this that the truly adventurous brands will tap into. One of the ways in which to connect a brand with its audience is to curate authentically their cultural and social needs, even if this means questioning the whole neoclassical economic platform from which the brand is sold. Even if it means questioning the brand itself. This may seem impossible, and to go against everything written in the brand bible, but it's a genuine way forward because, for the Unbrandables, honesty is indeed the best policy.

Most of us have been conditioned to accept brands as part of our day-to-day lives. The fact that we have become so used – immune, even – to the presence of global brands could be said to represent the greatest propaganda coup of the last fifty years. The creep of capitalism is embodied by the brands we encounter on a daily basis, and it's something that most people openly celebrate. Perhaps, however, we should be questioning this takeover. For many of us, brands have become extensions of our personalities, visual shortcuts to something we want to communicate (think fashion, cars, technology). As this overload continues, it could well reach a point where brands become meaningless, and the only reaction then would be to become un-branded, to de-brand. This is when the brand must mutate to the next level.

Culture and consumerism have almost become one and the same. A decade ago, A-list movie stars would never have chosen to be the face of a brand (although some of them undertook campaigns in the Far East that no one in the West would ever see, *Lost in Translation* style). Today, George Clooney sells instant coffee and Iggy Pop – once the doyen of heroin-soaked counter-culture – shifts car insurance. This is an important watermark on the cultural landscape, left by the sea of brands: when our heroes cash out and grab the flag of commerce, what do we do next? To understand why people are beginning to turn their backs on brands, we have to understand how brands have become part of the social fabric. And then, more importantly, we have to look at what people are turning to instead, in order to fill the cultural void. Culture is, after all, an important part of a balanced, healthy society.

'I don't think the customer is king. I think we're like a client sitting in a restaurant and we've been handed a menu, and we've got new informational tools these days to find out what is really on that menu. But our greatest power is not in choosing between items on a menu. Real power is in choosing what gets on that menu.'

Annie Leonard, sustainability champion

What's driving this rejection of mass consumption and global culture, of brand worship, is a desire for something real. After a decade or so of digital dreams and online experiences, people are beginning to crave something worthwhile, something substantial. This growing body of individuals who refuse to be sold to appears to have no respect (or use) for global brands. They refuse to be led, cajoled or persuaded to stray from their chosen path. They also reject the conventions of modern life – the nine-to-five – with many of them having opted out of the rat race. Demographically speaking, they are the 'homeless', wandering the earth in their search for an authentic, meaningful life, for substance. But this means that they've become a demographic in their own right, one that, however subtly or brand-frugally, still consumes. They still buy stuff. The problem is that these folks don't fall into any existing advertising category – until now, that is. They are the Unbrandables.

The subject of alternative lifestyles raises an immediate question: where do the Unbrandables get their money from? They have to have money or they wouldn't even be on the radar, and no brand or business would take an interest in how they lived. OK, so some of them are high-income professionals who have dropped out with a healthy bank balance, but increasingly they are the over-forties who never opted in and whose ability to spend is severely limited. Many of them rely on inheritances and trust-funds (however small), on benefits, on grey-area and illegal commerce, on bartering their skills for goods, on loopholes and scams. Some just have several jobs. This makes it even more important what they spend their money on, as it's hard earned and not easily come by.

'The conscious and intelligent manipulation of the organized habits and opinions of the masses is an important element in democratic society. Those who manipulate this unseen mechanism of society constitute an invisible government, which is the true ruling power of our country. We are governed, our minds are moulded, our tastes formed, our ideas suggested, largely by men we have never heard of. This is a logical result of the way in which our democratic society is organized.'

Edward Bernays, PR pioneer, 1928

This book has three main strands. First of all, I attempt to define the world of the new brand space. Secondly, I set out on a journey to meet those people and visit those places that are, by definition, Unbrandable. Thirdly, I look at the ways in which brands have to behave if they want to succeed in this new market, as well as examining the brands that are ahead of the curve. The Unbrandables may appear to be decidedly anti-brand, but they still consume, albeit in a very different way to the rest of the brand-hungry world. What makes them tick? How do you interact with them? How do you grab the attention of, connect with and, ultimately, make a sale to a global tribe who resolutely refuse to grow up, sell out, settle for less or slow down? I look at the lives and the stories of the Unbrandables, and at the brands that have managed to get through their armour, to work out who, what, when, where and why. Hold on tight: this one is going to be a bit different.

#55
Moments in Unbrandable Time

#1
Unbranded Brands: The Beastie Boys

Let's kick this off with three guys for whom I have massive amounts of love and respect: three artists from New York who started out as a punk band and ended up as one of the biggest alternative – yet influential – hip-hop acts on the planet. The Beastie Boys are now one of the coolest Unbrandable brands out there, not only because they have succeeded in attracting fans of all ages (thanks to the way in which they constantly reinvent themselves), but also because of the political and spiritual beliefs of the late Adam Yauch, aka MCA. Word of his death from cancer in 2012 at the age of forty-seven was international news, but even bigger was the splash made when it was revealed that his last will and testament includes a clause that forbids anyone from using his music, likeness or any art he's created in connection with hawking products. This certainly took the Beastie Boys into the realm of the Unbrandables. I'm probably going to get some stick for referring to them as a brand, but that is what they have become, albeit a glorious example of one that embodies the undiluted spirit of rebellion.

'The idea was "let's start a hardcore band", kind of as a joke.' This was MCA in 1998, speaking to *Spin* magazine. 'We called it the Beastie Boys. We were trying to think of the stupidest name, something that maybe sounded like the Angry Samoans.' Ironically, the Beastie Boys got their first break when British Airways sampled a portion of their song 'Beastie Revolution' (1983) in a commercial without seeking permission, an act that resulted in the Beasties winning $40,000 in damages. 'That money enabled us to make the move for independence', recalled the band's Mike D (Michael Diamond) in the same interview. 'We got a floor in this Chinese sweatshop building on Chrystie Street.' It was in this apartment that they lived, rehearsed and recorded their early work, swiftly moving from punk rock to hip hop, buying cheap Chinese knock-off Adidas tracksuits from a shop downstairs at a time when Grandmaster Flash and the Sugar Hill Gang were becoming more and more popular, off the back of the growing hip-hop movement (graffiti, breakdancing, MC-ing, DJ-ing). Through their friendship with the producer Rick Rubin, the Beastie Boys were introduced to Russell Simmons, with whom Rick had just started the legendary record label Def Jam Recordings. Russell spotted something unique in the three Jewish boys in a very black world, and introduced them to Run DMC and Public Enemy. 'The Beastie Boys are one of the key ingredients for spreading rap to suburbia', explained Public Enemy's Chuck D in 1998. 'They did it with their own flavour; they didn't, like, compromise who they were.'

The Beasties broke through to the mainstream when they toured the world with their debut album, *Licensed to Ill* (1986), the first rap album to reach number one in the *Billboard* chart. The band soon caught the eye of the tabloid press, which railed against them in the name of decency (a bit of a joke, really, when you think of the phone-jacking scandal and general sneakiness of the gutter press; 'Pop Idols Sneer at Dying Kids' was the lie of one headline in the *Daily Mirror*) and told the middle classes to lock up their daughters. *Licensed to Ill* was made as a joke, a pastiche of American frat culture – beers and strippers and partying – but this didn't stop the millions of people who bought the record and saw the band tour from believing that this was what the Beasties were really about. Both musically and culturally, it was the band's second album, *Paul's Boutique* (1989), that cemented their place in history. Miles Davis said that he never tired of listening to the album, which says it all if you ask me. The album bombed commercially, as the fans of their first record just didn't get it, but soon the rest of the world began to listen. Today, it is recognized as one of the greatest hip-hop records of all time. What a journey.

The Beastie Boys brand worked because:

1. musically, they never stood still, mutating from punk to hip hop to thrash to jazz to hip hop again;

2 they rapped about what they knew – being white boys, chasing girls and smoking weed;

3 they oozed authentic 'fight the power' attitude;

4 they didn't care about working with brands (although they unconsciously aligned themselves to Adidas in almost every photo shoot) before creating their own: Grand Royal and Oscilloscope Laboratories.

#2
Unbrandable People: Marylin Cayrac

Marylin, a photographer, first contacted me after buying one of my books: 'You need to know that *Street Knowledge* [2010] is my bible. I admire what you do, what you've done. I wish I could live and eat thanks to my passions, which are street art and underground culture. Of course, I haven't seen much about either as I am eighteen years old and live in the south of France. But I travel when I can, and try to find what people can't see.' Since then I have done everything I can to help her, including featuring a couple of her photos in my last book. I liked her open and honest attitude, and after I got to know her a bit (in the digital world, as we've never met in real life) I knew she would be the first Unbrandable person in this book.

'To me,' says Marylin, 'a product is something you can touch, feel or buy if you need it. A brand is just an idea of the product. The majority of brands are so known right now that we don't even call things by their name; we just say their brands. We are just knocked out by all the commercials, and aren't even capable of thinking above them. If we were able to think a little, maybe we would stop giving money to the same people every time! Those people who don't give a shit about us, after all. I don't even think I have any brand that I'm particularly loyal to, but that may be a bit hypocritical. I may have a touch, as I like some photographers' touches, some styles that I want to copy, to acquire. I don't know, I like clean shit. Weird, sinister, grey landscapes. Or sad portraits. That's what reaches me.

'I cannot live without some brands. I admire those people who decide to live in a forest or on a farm and can provide for themselves. I would love to do that, but right now I live in a city to study, and money leads my life. As it does with a lot of people. In my own small way, all I can do to avoid liberalism and capitalism is to get some old furniture for my flat, buy some vegetables from local producers … But that's ridiculous. I work on an Apple MacBook, my underwear comes from H&M, and I drive to school every day. I am money-dependent. But I don't like it.'

#3
Define 'Brand'

'I believe brands are becoming much more personal. We're moving from broadcasting to narrowcasting. And if you've got a good story then people will listen, and if it's bloody boring then they're not going to. That's the market, that's the Internet: give me your story. You're as good as the energy you give out. It's about who you really are, and that's what people are looking for – authenticity, genuine stories. We're looking for someone who's going to share something genuine with us that we love, that makes us laugh and get up and slam the table and sink another beer. But that requires courage. It requires the will to fail, the absence of fear – in other words, love. It requires that people love their customers, and it requires that they remove the illusion of separation. We are not separate from our customers, we are a part of them.

Invite your customer into your brand, into your building. Understand that you're casting a spell – we are the wizards of the modern age, us brand marketers. It's about having a good story, putting that story out there, and getting people involved in it, and it's useful if that story also happens to be true. People mistakenly think it's about branding and messaging. It's about who you really are. They will sniff you out, and if you are not telling the truth then they will drop you like a bad habit. The only two questions

any company needs to ask are: what's our point
and why should people care? If those questions are
answered with a narrative that's involving and inspiring
and interesting then you've got something. If they're
not then you gotta think harder, as all you've really
got is a product.'

BJ Cunningham, propagandist

There is little doubt that brands have become extremely powerful.
But as their power is often seen in a negative light, this isn't necessarily
a good thing. If you ask me, however, in an ideal world such power
presents a glorious opportunity to do something for the good, for
the great – a subject I'll examine in more detail later in the book. But
acknowledging how powerful brands have become also throws up a
number of questions: is our obsession with brands the result of a cheap
trick? Is a brand a set of cognitive associations linked to something
or someone, or is it just a physical object? Is there anywhere in the
world that has not been infiltrated by the brand?

So many questions, so little time.

There are brands and there are products: this is the defining line.
A brand is something that we have an emotional connection with. It may
be completely fake and manufactured, but we nevertheless experience
some kind of bond. This is human programming at its best. It takes a
certain something to evoke in a prospective consumer a sudden feeling
of connection when he or she is stood in the supermarket at 7.30 p.m.
after a hard day's work, hungry as a horse, looking for something half-
decent to chow but faced with a shelf of identical brands. 'Which ready
meal do I buy?' The brand that pulls at our heartstrings – like a puppy
at the pound – is the brand that will get our money. Ker-ching!

**'[A brand] is a collection of concepts that have been
put into a formal vehicle in order to market and sell
and transmit either goods or services from a collective**

corporation to a collective recipient ... Any company is a brand, although any person could be a brand – once they get any kind of notoriety they become a brand. It needs a tribe; it needs a certain mass in order for it to break through as a brand.'

Denzyl Feigelson, Music Synergist, iTunes

The way I see it is that because everything in the cultural world is constantly changing, brands have to adapt to these changes in order to remain relevant. This dynamic relationship to culture, however, is something that the world of brands rarely celebrates. For brands to admit that what really makes them attractive is all the stuff that has rubbed off on to them from the world of culture is way too honest, way to close to the knuckle. But this is what makes a successful brand story stand out. A company creates a product – a sneaker, say – but the real gravity and magnetism of that product is created by the culture that embraces it. In other words, it's not the brand that made the sneaker cool, but culture. This fact is a game changer, but once the brand story becomes the focus of all communications, nothing can get in its way, regardless of the real story, regardless of the truth.

'[Companies] see culture as an investment, as a kind of intellectual property that they can get a return on, because that's the only way the accountants can account for it. But we know that there is this much softer thing at play, and that's actually a much more powerful thing. And that is the bit that you can't really brand. That's the human bit, the bit we can't disagree with; it's the truth. What's the value of MTV? It's the eyeballs that watch it. The consumers. Facebook – it's the people on it, right? And again, this is part of the equation, and I don't think we're going to be rethinking that anytime soon. But the bittersweet

thing is that brands can become so successful that they forget about the people who made them successful in the first place. Or they make themselves so desirable that they create their own problems.'

Jeremy Brown, founder and CEO, Sense Worldwide

So let's forget the mirages that advertising agencies and marketing departments build around brands. The global rise of many brands is indelibly linked to underground cultural phenomena, and this is the real juice, the real deal. It's also the kind of thing that gets me out of bed each day. But it's strange how global brands often behave as though they are made of kryptonite one moment and glass the next – saturating the media one day and then censoring it twenty-four hours later if anyone has anything to say that isn't 100 per cent complimentary. One thing, however, is certain: the way in which brands acquire their market share is never by simply being the best, as all products out there are pretty much identical. To quote Malcolm X remixing Jean-Paul Sartre, they do it 'by any means necessary'.

In one way or another we are all brands, and behave as such. From the current crop of hipsters running around the planet to the yummy mummies of Stoke Newington, Westchester and Prenzlauer Berg, we are all self-branded by the choices we make everyday – by the cars we drive, the clothes we wear, the food we eat, and so on. And what we display in public we extend into the digital realm via our social-media channels. I think a lot of us are totally unaware of this fact, and so our 'brand' is pretty shite: photos of getting wasted, misbehaving, hating/ trolling, duck-faces, trying to look 'sexy', wearing something hideous, driving an expensive yet ridiculous-looking car – all of which damages 'brand me'. Image, after all, is everything, and the power of the brand is controlled by its story, its choices and its image. The key ingredient in these three elements is authenticity. If it's an authentic choice then it will work for the brand and it will work for us.

So here is my definition: a brand is a thing or a person or a company that has got some kind of media traction and has managed (by hook or by crook) to get itself on the public radar and into our heads. The first rule for any brand is that we all have to know about it; we have to be aware that it exists, as only then can it begin to build its story deep within our subconscious. The second rule is that it has to offer something in return (apart from the actual product) for either our money or our loyalty. This is where it gets interesting. Thanks to the digital revolution, cultural currency has become almost as important as the regular, physical, common or garden dollar or pound, because it all helps to drive the story of the product – the all-important backstory – into the mind of the consumer.

#4
Unbranded Brands: Phonebloks

As we all know, most mobile phones last a couple of years before they slow down or stop working altogether (that's if you haven't already broken it) – a great example of planned obsolescence in full effect. In most cases it's one small part of the phone that has actually broken, but because of the way in which they're designed, you can't just swap that part for a new one. Until now, that is. The Phoneblok is a mobile phone designed around a system of detachable components, or 'bloks', connected to a solid base that locks them all together. If a certain blok breaks, you simply replace it; and if the phone is slowing down, you can upgrade the processor for a faster one. All this revolves around the Blokstore, a digital hub where you can buy, sell, read reviews, get information or just purchase a ready-assembled phone. The tagline is 'A Phone Worth Keeping'.

The inventor of the Phoneblok is a chap called Dave Hakkens, a designer from the Netherlands whose goal is to make the world a better place by making things that can be fixed and not just thrown away – better and sustainable things. He started this quest when his beloved digital camera stopped working. After trying to fix it himself, he discovered that the one part he needed was not available anywhere. Dave was also acutely aware of waste streams (the total flow of waste from manufacture to disposal) generated by the mobile-phone industry, so he started working on a phone that could be easily fixed and would not contribute to these waste streams. Phonebloks was born, and has since gathered considerable digital momentum – a social-media reach of more than 380 million people. The first major company to get on board was Motorola. The Google-owned telecommunications giant had been working on its own modular phone, and approached Phonebloks asking if it could get involved. As Dave wants Phonebloks to become a reality, he agreed, but with the strict condition that the consumer must always be kept in the loop, so that the project can be developed in the open. To me, Phonebloks represents an authentic link between producer and consumer. This is something that really needs to be focused on – how brands can genuinely connect with the consumer. Motorola's involvement with Phonebloks tells me that the once-blinkered eyes of the tech giants are slowly beginning to open.

'We are the most excited about our new way of working. Usually companies don't share their ideas until they are ready for market. Phonebloks believes the world should be involved during development. Due to the huge amount of support on Phonebloks we were able to inspire Motorola and "open up" the project sooner than planned. It's quite a new step in how products are developed on this scale. In this way the entire Phonebloks community is looking over the shoulders of Motorola to make sure everything goes according to plan. We believe this will keep the project on the right course.'

Dave Hakkens, founder, Phonebloks

Why Phonebloks works:

1. The product fills a technological need.
2. It comes from an honest place – no planned obsolescence.
3. It is ecologically sound – no excess waste.
4. The creators and the brand are very accessible.
5. It has a positive identity.

#5
A Short History of Mass-Marketing

Edward Bernays, who we heard from at the beginning, is generally regarded as the inventor of PR, the first form of mass-market advertising. After helping Woodrow Wilson lead the American public into the First World War – under the banner not of restoring the old empires, but of bringing democracy to Europe – Bernays realized that 'if you could use propaganda for war, you could certainly use it for peace'. But thanks to the German war effort, propaganda had acquired a bad name, so Bernays coined the term 'public relations' and set up the first advertising agency just off Broadway.

As a consequence of the war, the United States had become a heavily industrialized society with millions of people living in cities, and Bernays wanted to influence the way these masses thought and felt. After reading a book written by his uncle – *A General Introduction to Psychoanalysis* (1915) by Sigmund Freud – Bernays realized that he could make money for his clients by manipulating the public's unconscious. Bernays's insight was that behaviour is not driven by information; instead, it's all about repressed desires and animal instincts. He realized that if he could link products to desires and emotions, he could influence what people bought. He was thus the first person to create an emotional connection between consumer and product – something that is still in use today.

Up until then, products were sold purely on the basis of the market's needs, but the corporations – which controlled the manufacturing of goods, and which were represented by Bernays – knew that they had to alter this state of affairs in order to sell as fast as they could produce. Bernays's theories helped change the basis of the public's buying habits from needs to desires: 'Man's desires must overshadow his needs', as Paul Mazur of Lehman Brothers wrote in 1927. The corporations also needed the public to be conditioned into wanting new products before the old ones had been fully consumed. This, then, was the birth of planned obsolescence. Fast forward ninety years and this is one of Apple's core philosophies.

Through such innovations as product placement in Hollywood movies and the selling of cars as symbols of male sexuality, Bernays succeeded in convincing the American public to buy products not because they needed them but in order to express their inner selves. By the late 1920s Americans had shifted from being citizens to being consumers: what really mattered now was buying stuff. As governments realized to their delight, it was consumerism that drove life, that kept the public happy. Provided the people were busy living, working and buying, those in charge could be left alone to pursue other interests.

It was the philosopher, sociologist and political theorist Herbert Marcuse who spotted that consumerism had become a form of social control. 'The people recognize themselves in their commodities', he wrote in 1964. 'They find their soul in their automobile, hi-fi set, split-level home, kitchen equipment. The very mechanism which ties the individual to his society has changed, and social control is anchored in the new needs which it has produced.' The students that Marcuse taught – at Columbia, Harvard, Brandeis University and the University of California, San Diego – picked up on this way of thinking, and soon the protest movement was born, railing against the control of corporate America. Its members quickly understood that the most effective form of protest was to regain control of their own minds and free themselves from state and corporate hegemony. The way forward was for the public to talk about the things that the state wanted repressed.

This movement led to the creation of the cult of the self. The Unbrandable reference point here is that these new thinkers were still consumers, but what they wanted were products and brands that expressed their individuality – that would make them stand out as different in a conformist society and marketplace. The corporations were caught napping, and it took them a decade or so to catch up, to tap into this new demographic. Enter the focus group, which, by the 1980s, was how the corporations discovered not only how their brands were perceived but also what they should be producing. The generation that once rebelled against consumerism was now fully embedded in it.

The history of mass-marketing appears to be cyclical in nature, a pendulum swinging back and forth. There will always be someone stood opposite, reacting against the current position, but eventually that person's counter-position will become the norm – the way stuff is then sold. Once this is understood, we can look at where the market is right now and then swing across to the opposite, the antithesis. This is the starting point for the Unbrandable solution.

#6
Unbranded Brands: Fat Willy's Surf Shack

Fat Willy's Surf Shack is a British institution. Which is a bit of an oxymoron, when you think about it: how often do you see the words 'British' and 'surf' in the same sentence? But therein lies the germ of something original. Born in Newquay in Cornwall – the centre of the UK surf industry – and still going strong after thirty years with the same logo, Fat Willy's Surf Shack produces T-shirts, sweatshirts and hoodies (keeping it simple) that are worn all over the world, from Newquay to Barbados.

Back in the day, having run various businesses in Northamptonshire – from a plumber's to a greengrocer's to a market stall selling clothes – Fat Willy's founder Roger Ward discovered iron-on T-shirt transfers in the United States and began flying in an out of New York every fortnight and filling his suitcase with the things. Eventually, he had enough of them to open up a shop in Kettering where you could have a T-shirt printed with a design of your choice. Genius.

Fat Willy's is now run by Roger's son, Chris, who picks up the story of the company's birth. 'For some reason,' he explains, 'my dad decided to open a similar shop in Newquay, Cornwall – despite it being 300 miles from where we lived – where he believed the transfers would prove very popular with tourists. Soon, we had a T-shirt shop in Newquay as well as a T-shirt printing business in Kettering, where we printed garments for local schools, clubs and fashion shops. It was then he decided to create his own T-shirt designs for his Newquay shop within the fledgling surfing industry but aimed at tourists.'

Roger came up with several designs – 'Surf Rats', 'Fair Do's Surf Shirts', 'Pink Lady', 'Tropical Sunrise' – but one in particular, designed in 1984, proved more popular than the rest: 'Fat Willy's Surf Shack'. 'To this day,' says Chris, 'I'm not sure where the inspiration came from. But he had a vision of a three-colour paint-effect logo in the neon colours popular in the eighties – a beach shack complete with real bamboo, palm trees, jukebox, animated birds and monkeys!'

The original 'shack' was at the back of the Newquay shop: a bit of sand, some cans of Foster's lying around and a bamboo wall with the Fat Willy's Surf Shack T-shirt displayed on it. This T-shirt soon became the most popular item in the shop, and then the whole shop became a shack. Then the brand tipped over into the mainstream.

'I distinctly remember one summer when I was seventeen working in the Newquay shop,' recalls Chris, 'with queues of people waiting for it to open. There were times when the shop was so packed you couldn't see across it. "Large black" was the most sought-after size and style, and a simple trip to the stockroom would be like a rugby scrum – and you'd have none left before you reached the counter! It was a good few years. Sadly, it didn't last long. A brutal recession in the early nineties, coupled with rapid expansion and more than a few bad partners, almost put the company under. However, we just survived and tried to get rid of many of the underperforming shops (and the partners) in other locations.'

This is something to remember when creating a brand: don't rinse it! Street art, raves, skating – all subcultures that tipped over into the mainstream and got ruined by people jumping on board just to make money. I've never seen anything resembling a Fat Willy's advert or marketing campaign, but I've seen a million T-shirts sporting the neon logo that never seems to change. Today, Fat Willy's is synonymous with Newquay and Cornwall, which is the ultimate achievement for any brand: to become part of the vernacular.

Why Fat Willy's works:

1 As a brand it's consistent, reliable, honest and uncomplicated.
2 The business is family-run and -owned.
3 'Fat Willy's' has entered the language of surfing.

#7
Product vs Brand

'A product is just a functional "thing" that you can buy. A brand is the personality of the product. A brand adds a layer of emotion and meaning that users can identify with – or not. Since nowadays most products are much alike, brands become increasingly important for differentiation.'

Onno Lixenberg, cookie-baker and adman

The difference between brand and product is that the brand is loved. Seriously. People actually feel something for it, deep down inside. Writing these words seems completely crazy, as brands are just things we buy. And yet, as we have seen, they also inspire emotional connections. On a personal note, I have trouble working with brands I don't get or care about. I dislike big, nasty brands (fast foods, banks, soft drinks, pharmaceuticals, etc.) as much as the next bloke, but deep down I am indelibly marked by the brands that shaped my cultural DNA. Converse, Stüssy, Canon, Lacoste, Sergio Tacchini, Rolex, Vans, MDMA, Sony. But as these particular brands are relevant only to my story, I can't really tell anyone to buy them or try to convince them that they need these things in their lives. When I work with brands all I can do is project my story into the space (hopefully) occupied by the brand.

To return to the definition of a brand: for a brand to function successfully in the marketplace, it has to behave properly. This means treating its customers and their interests – their hobbies and their passions – with the utmost respect. And it has to do all of these things without asking for anything in return. So yes, the brand has to be 100 per cent authentic. Products, on the other hand, don't do any of this. Products are just all up in our faces at every opportunity – think of car or household insurance. We all really hate them, but still they roll on down the hill towards us.

'Sell them their dreams. Sell them what they longed for and hoped for and almost despaired of having. Sell them hats by splashing sunlight across them. Sell them dreams – dreams of country clubs and proms and visions of what might happen if only ... After all, people don't buy things to have things. They buy things to work for them. They buy hope – hope of what your merchandise will do for them. Sell them this hope and you won't have to worry about selling them goods.'

Helen Landon Cass, radio personality, 1923

At some point, there was a shift from selling something physical to selling an idea. A dream. A lifestyle. Nike went from producing and selling running shoes to practically owning the whole concept of sport, especially in the younger, more youthful urban space. Likewise, Red Bull went from buying the European rights to a Thai energy drink to owning extreme sports. This is the ultimate in branding a product: 'owning' something that no one can really claim as their own. Like nature. Or laughter. To boil it right down, a product is something that is bought because there is no way round it. No other choice. Petrol, medicine, insurance, basic food stuffs. We may not want to buy any of these, but we have to.

The backlash against brands has a lot to do with the infiltration of product and brand advertising into every available space. It's an obvious statement to make, but this is where it began, with the force-feeding of brand communications that didn't even pretend to care about the world – or us, for that matter. All they cared about was making money and shifting units. The rise of the product is scary stuff, especially from an ecological perspective, and part of the motivation of the Unbrandables is to remove or block out the visual pollution that has crept into the cities of the world.

'One of the PR triumphs of the twenty-first century was the rise of Barack Obama. His campaign slogan was "change we can believe in". He was a brand that offered something special, exciting. In 2008 Obama the candidate was voted marketer of the year, ahead of Apple, Nike and Coors Beer. He made many people feel good, as if his slogan might be true. Above all the perception of Brand Obama was that he was against war. But that was false. As president, Obama has … backed US military action in Afghanistan, Pakistan, Somalia and Yemen. And approved a military budget of $708 billion, the biggest war spending of all time.'

John Pilger, journalist, writer and film-maker

But a brand is nothing without its disciples. If a brand doesn't look after them or embrace them or listen to them, then it will lose them. No brand is bigger than its customers, but quite a few of them think and behave as if they are. When the customer says 'Jump', the brand has to ask not only 'How high?' but also 'Is there anything else I can do for you?' (to quote the employees of John Lewis). A brand can avoid all this hassle, however, by doing the research into the lives of its customers properly, at the beginning, and then using these insights to help it act and behave in an authentic, transparent way. Decent, like. It may sound strange, but brands have to behave like people in order to grow. And this brings us back to the difference between product and brand: when you look at a brand, you see some kind of personality and not just a pie sitting on a chiller shelf. This humanizes an inanimate object and creates a link with the customer. A brand has the ability to create a popular product because of its identity, but only if it has reached a critical mass, and only if there is an authentic connection with the customer. This connection is usually forged in a genuine moment of discovery, what I like to call a 'fuck me' moment (as documented in *The Stuff You Can't Bottle*). These moments, which can include the discovery not only of products but also of such intangibles as whole music scenes, make a huge difference to which brands are liked, loved – and even worshipped.

'The club was down some dingy backstreet by the docks. From the outside it was not what I was expecting. Nothing could have prepared me for what I was about to witness inside the club. The place was rammed. The clientele were almost all black, all male and very gay. The club was made up of numerous rooms; it was impossible to get any idea of how big the place actually was as it was so chock-full and difficult to get around. This was like no nightclub that I had ever been in before. The unseen sound system was pumping out tune after tune of which I'd never heard the like before. Mainly they were stripped-back extended mixes of shuddering electro tracks with soul divas' voices on top; they almost made the Giorgio Moroder records I knew sound like kids' stuff. Track after track, all seamlessly segueing into one another. Never a drop in the energy level. This was something else altogether. It was literally an ocean away from cheesy Euro disco or the soul-boy sounds that dance clubs would have been playing in the UK … On leaving the place I noticed that it was called the Paradise Garage.'

Bill Drummond, musician, artist and writer

#8
Unbranded Brands:
Village Voice

Manhattan – especially downtown – has changed beyond belief in the last twenty years, but there has at least been one constant amid all this flux: the *Village Voice*. Established in 1955, this free weekly newspaper features investigative articles, analysis of current affairs, coverage of the arts and events listings for New York City; '10 Things To Do Under $10' caught my eye last time I read it. It tells it like it is and has a very loyal following, and for me it's an integral part of both the physical and the cultural landscape of Manhattan. More importantly, perhaps, the *Voice* (as it's known locally) offers a virtual 'place' for the Unbrandables to congregate. It's also culturally embedded in the downtown scene of the late 1970s and early 1980s, which is something you just can't manufacture.

The words of many legends have been published in the *Voice*. One of its founders was Norman Mailer, while its many contributors include Katherine Anne Porter, Tom Stoppard, Allen Ginsberg and Lorraine Hansberry. Quentin Crisp used to write the film reviews, and in October 2013, during his month-long city-wide residency, 'Better Out Than In', Banksy gave the *Voice* an exclusive interview, some of which was so Unbrandable it hurt:

Village Voice: What was your vision for 'Better Out Than In', and how and why the project was conceived?
Banksy: There is absolutely no reason for doing this show at all. I know street art can feel increasingly like the marketing wing of an art career, so I wanted to make some art without the price tag attached.

There's no gallery show or book or film. It's pointless. Which hopefully means something.

Village Voice: And where and when will the new pieces be installed?

Banksy: The plan is to live here, react to things, see the sights – and paint on them. Some of it will be pretty elaborate, and some will just be a scrawl on a toilet wall.

Village Voice: Have you abandoned totally the idea of showing in galleries?

Banksy: I started painting on the street because it was the only venue that would give me a show; now I have to keep painting on the street to prove to myself it wasn't a cynical plan. Plus it saves money on having to buy canvases. But there's no way round it – commercial success is a mark of failure for a graffiti artist. We're not supposed to be embraced in that way. When you look at how society rewards so many of the wrong people, it's hard not to view financial reimbursement as a badge of self-serving mediocrity.

The secret formula of the *Village Voice*:

1. Impeccable cultural heritage
2. A lone, independent voice in a sea of co-opted/bought media
3. Stays true to its roots but moves with the times

#9
Words with the Shaman: Jeremy Brown

Not long ago, my brother-in-law Irvin emailed me to say that during his commute home on the M60 he had heard a guy talking on the radio about people living off the grid. Knowing the kind of thing I was into, he reckoned I should check it out. So I went online, listened to the feature on the BBC iPlayer – and liked what I heard. Jeremy Brown runs an innovation, strategy and insight company called Sense Worldwide, which grew out of an informal network of like-minded people influenced (as I was) by the prevailing culture of late 1980s London: Stüssy, hip hop, skateboarding, house and techno club the Brain, streetwear, raving, cheap flights to New York and Los Angeles, and emerging technology. I got in touch with Jeremy, and when we were both in the same city we started hanging out together. What came next was a masterclass in brands, the future of brands and how to glean relevant and authentic insights.

An important indicator of Jeremy's approach to brands is his initial scepticism about the title of this book. 'When we first started the business ten years ago', he explains, 'the whole noise was around Naomi Klein's *No Logo* [1999] and the whole premise it set out. And I think it's one of those things – I could set the argument out on both sides of the fence.' On one side, he explains, he could say that brands have never been more important than they are today, while on the other, he could put forward the idea that they're redundant. Kaput. 'I think really what differentiates the two [arguments] is essentially the values on which a company is built, that are sitting behind the brand, or the brand itself, depending on what it is. I see this time and time again … and certainly in this world with the Web. I'm talking about the different sorts of shifts that we've been through.'

Like many of us older folk, Jeremy grew up in an analogue world. That didn't stop him, however, from realizing that a massive change was coming. In the early 1990s he predicted that people were 'going to have to retrain. It doesn't matter what your degree is in now, there is going to be a whole different approach to how we do business and how we learn stuff and all the rest of it.' He was also one of the first people to realize that when you're dealing with a brand, the bottom line is all about values – about knowing who you are, what you stand for and, most importantly, where you fit in. One of the first pieces of work carried out by Sense Worldwide was something for Proctor & Gamble called a 'management learning module'. 'The title was "Working with Culture",' explains Jeremy, 'because that's how far we've come. We've gone from brands that have had to run and catch up and understand the cultural context that they are working in, to now when you've seen the rise of streetwear and all of those brands. That was probably the first thing that really woke me up. You've got to look at the whole DIY culture that was around: you had the graphic-design businesses, people getting up and doing their own thing, but there was a set of values.' And it was out of these values that a different understanding of how a brand could exist was born.

Inevitably, talk turns to consumption and the fact that most people don't like change, which is why – even though he works in research – Jeremy has never held a focus group. 'I've always favoured working with the people more at the extremes. It's often people at the extremes who are already living in the future, somehow – they're out there.' One of the people he's worked with is a young woman in her twenties who lives a completely self-sufficient life in a caravan, in a wood somewhere in Dorset: 'She has dropped off the gird – no electricity, and that is just her thing.' The reason Jeremy's interested in working with such people is that they tend to be very articulate, and are therefore able to talk about why they've opted out and what they're doing to remove themselves from the system. 'And that's where you can go to get the inspiration and bring some of those ideas back into the mainstream, because these guys really are like the trailblazers.' Often, when we talk about people at the cutting edge, we're talking about people obsessed with music, fashion and technology. But this fails to take into account all the other aspects of life. Most research follows the money, but where we should be going is to a place of little money, fashion or technology. Back to the beginning. 'And often that's where those great ideas are lurking', says Jeremy. 'Certainly for me, that's the piece. William Gibson said, "The future is already here, it's just not that well distributed yet". And it's those people at the edges – it's where the future is, for me. And those are my friends, those are the people I have some strange attraction to.'

It's all very well for us to talk about people 'off the grid', but I was interested in finding out how Jeremy actually tracks these people down. 'It's all been word of mouth', he explains. 'We intuitively created one of the first networks – a social network. No one even knew. When we were talking about an online social network, people stared at us blankly.' It wasn't until Malcolm Gladwell's *Tipping Point* was published in 2000 that people started asking Jeremy to tell them more about 'that thing you were talking to me about a year ago'. But he'd already moved on, and was thinking about how collaboration could lead to original insights. Then Facebook popped up, and Jeremy had already been there, done that – but without the branding. 'We were not a dot-com start-up, we were just a bunch of creative heads that knew that by bringing these diverse viewpoints together, those collisions would create transformations.' And when I looked at the friends Jeremy had when he was growing up, I found that they were from a wide variety of backgrounds – from gardening to art. 'All their ideas and perspectives were relevant – those people out at the edges.'

It's this peripheral area that Jeremy is most interested in now, especially when he's thinking about such challenges as how best to mesh contemporary culture with the corporate world, with the mainstream. 'Which leads us back to why I think brands can save the world, because they will not have a commission to operate unless they get their values right, and if they get their values right, they'll have a name. Everyone needs a name. Whether your brand is King Adz or Adam N. Stone it doesn't matter; it's just a different jacket you want to put around it, and as you're an individual you can do what you want. But I think the thing with brands is that it's the transparency piece of the puzzle that's so important.'

I ask Jeremy about what makes a brand work, and it turns out that he'd recently asked one of the interns at Sense to go through all the companies they work for and to summarize their core values. At the top of the list is Nike. 'I think they've now got it spot on', says Jeremy. 'They've been in trouble in the past, with sweatshops and all the rest of it …' Jeremy has done a fair amount of work for the Nike brand. 'I was talking to them about the idea that they just created the shoe – they are responsible for the genesis of the Dunk and the Air Force, etc., but it was culture that created the myth around them.' Without culture, in other words, a brand cannot accumulate any value or traction. OK, so a salesmen would go out and try to sell it, but the real gravity and magnetism of that product is created by the culture in which it operates. 'So don't think that you made that shoe cool: you made the shoe, and culture made it cool. And you can do stuff to be the catalyst, but to do that you have to know who you are, what you stand for and where you've got permission to fit in.'

In the brand world, everyone focuses on the successes. What they don't spend a whole lot of time thinking about are the failures. When Nike attempted to move into the world of extreme sports, for example, it assumed that all it had to do was sponsor some big surfing events, but it failed spectacularly. When a brand moves into a cultural space it has to be an organic thing, and the members of the extreme-sports culture – the surfers, the skiers, the divers, etc. – are not into the Nike brand at all. 'You have to build up the credibility', observes Jeremy. 'And yes, it was about sponsorship, but the reason skaters were getting sponsored in the early days was just to get them out of their shitty jobs so they could go and do what they love more. It wasn't about making them rich and larging it up. It was just allowing them to express themselves all the more.'

This is when our discussion gets interesting. We start to talk about brands doing good; brands as powerful forces that can change the world – something that I believe is central to the whole Unbrandables concept, but which for some is a contentious topic. Take Converse, for instance, which, although it's owned by Nike, sits at the opposite end of the spectrum to its parent company. (When you think about it, Nike are high-performance shoes for low-performance people, while Converse are low-performance shoes for high-performance people.) 'What Converse are doing with music is absolutely on the money', says Jeremy. 'They saved the 100 Club [a legendary music venue on Oxford Street in London], they saved that cultural Petri dish. They don't really promote it hard, but it gets them the respect they're due.' Across the pond in Brooklyn, New York, Converse has established a record studio called Rubber Tracks, where you can record your band for free and still retain the rights. 'They're fostering a culture that they can live in – and it's that symbiotic relationship. And that's where those investments go. Spend money on TV? I'm like, why? Its serving one machine, and that machine is broken. But it's what shareholders understand. And marketing people still don't have any influence in big companies.'

At the moment this is unlikely to change, or is changing rather slowly. Eventually, however (and this is pretty much what this book is all about), the bean counters, analysts and shareholders will begin to invest in this new space. 'And that's my point about viewing brands almost as little investments that you're making', observes Jeremy. 'Don't think about it as sinking a load of cash in TV and it's gone tomorrow. Now, is that good for business? Is that going to make me rich? No, probably not. But if the values are right and the purpose behind the brand is right … And when I talk about "the purpose", I mean what difference is that brand going to make to the world?'

As people who work with or examine brands and the cultures surrounding them, our purpose is to help make better things. It's as simple as that. And as we share this thought with more and more people, perhaps they will realize that this is a brilliant idea – that this is the way forward – and will get behind it and give it some momentum. 'That's how I'm going to rally the troops,' concludes Jeremy, 'and it's going to be creative thinkers and doers who are going to get us out of this shit. Whether they're scientists or whatever, it's the application of these ideas. For me, that's what it's all about.'

Sense Worldwide's summary of a successful brand:

1. Commitment to innovation and sustainability
2. Transparency is an asset not a risk

③ Collaboration enables systematic change

④ Every challenge and risk is an opportunity

⑤ Design allows you to prototype the future
rather than retrofit the past

⑥ To make a real change you have to be a catalyst

#10
Unbrandable Places: Berlin

Berlin, where paint bombs are hurled in protest at the speed of development, is one of the most Unbrandable cities in the world. Yes, a lot has changed – Kreuzberg used to be one of the coolest, most culturally diverse and cheapest parts of the city, and now it's one of the most expensive – but there are still pockets of resistance. I've been describing, filming and walking the streets of Berlin for many years now, and while I may have witnessed a change in its status from edgy outsider to affluent insider, I've also been aware of the constant presence of an alternative way of life. It's this ongoing opposition to globalization (and the brands that lead the charge) that makes the place so interesting. It gives it a soul, if that's possible. The uniqueness of the city is down to one thing: the mindset of its Unbrandable inhabitants.

'I'm happy that people are still protesting, otherwise we would live in an Ikea world. But I think it's more. It's a bigger phenomenon how the market has changed now [in 2013], with all this vertical change and with all these brands popping up, than to say, OK, that an alternative market is against everything mainstream. For me, it's the same – Berliners who protest that too many new apartments are being built because they don't like the way the city is developing, because it's too expensive for them to live in the city ... Come on, get a fucking life, then – because to worry about all

45

these things, you're not going to change it; it's just the way it is. Instead of hating and instead of kicking in doors, let's do something positive. Let's go for it and find another way in. Start your own thing if you are against it.'

Joey Elgersma, creative director

Berlin has become a hugely important incubator of subcultures, not to mention one of the busiest and fastest-growing places on the planet. This love of all things cultural is reflected, on a national scale, by the fact that Germany now has one of the highest-grossing book markets in the world, with more and more people reading books. It's these little indicators that have always caught my eye, such as when I discovered that one bookseller has more than 160 outlets in Israel – a lot of bookshops for a pretty small country. Back in Germany, it was the spaces in between the old East and West Berlin that I was always drawn to, the no-man's-land. When the Wall came down these spaces became testaments to a previous era. And with space in a city a rare thing indeed, they are now being developed at an amazing rate.

'I try to follow the various phenomena that have influenced my personal life. For example, in the early 1990s the combination of free and available space after the Wall came down, and the new age of electronic and techno music, was fascinating. I began to go to clubs, and then ended up running a club, and all along I was photographing these places. I still photograph the people, mostly musicians, who I met ten or fifteen years ago as the contemporary performers they still are today.'

Martin Eberle, photographer

Why Berlin works:

In many places around the world you will find people working outside the mainstream, creating and producing their own fashion, music, art and film. There are a lot of these kinds of people living and working in Berlin, crafting things to sell in order to support their dreams – probably because it has long been seen as a cheap, youthful place to live. This alternative movement is now an integral and acknowledged part of the city.

#11
Unbranded Brands: In-N-Out Burger

People who refuse even to talk about McDonald's or Burger King or KFC, let alone eat in one of their restaurants, still have a soft spot for In-N-Out Burger. It's a funny one, all right, especially when you think about fast food's (often deserved) reputation for terrible food (lips and bits), a high turnover of staff and poor working conditions – for being an industry, basically, that just doesn't care. A lot of the time this is true; think about the 'McLibel case' in the UK, often referred to as the biggest corporate PR disaster in history. Over the years the fast-food industry has given the impression that it thinks it can bully its way out of trouble, without any kind of retribution, perhaps because it knows that there will always be a demand for fast food, that litigation or a bad reputation won't diminish people's hunger. But with In-N-Out Burger, a regional chain of fast-food restaurants founded in California in 1948, the story is slightly different.

'Lunchtime at the flagship In-N-Out Burger restaurant in Baldwin Park, California, is a study in efficiency. As the order line swells, smiling workers swoop in to operate empty cash registers. Another staffer cleans tables, asking customers if they're enjoying their hamburger. Outside, a woman armed with a hand-held ordering machine speeds up the drive-through line ... New store openings often resemble product releases from Apple Inc., with customers lined up hours in advance. City officials plead with the Irvine, California-based company to open restaurants in their municipalities.'

Seth Lubove, journalist

For me, having a fast-food brand in this book is the ultimate proof of the rise of the Unbrandables. What makes In-N-Out Burger such an Unbrandable brand is its philosophy of looking after its customers and making sure they've got the best product (in terms of both their health and their wallet). It's all about going that extra mile.

'First and foremost I'd like to thank my grandfather and grandmother, Harry and Esther Snyder. Their vision, passion and commitment set such a firm foundation for our company, and the core values that they established for us back in 1948 still guide us today. My grandfather was an incredibly hard worker who was passionate about quality. Back in the day, he hand-selected only the highest quality meat, cheese and produce for his customers. My grandmother was always right there with her husband from the start, equally committed to quality and always making sure the In-N-Out Associates were treated like family. Additionally, she was the driving force behind In-N-Out's philanthropic efforts and today, the In-N-Out Burgers Foundation still carries out her vision. I'd also like to thank my uncle Rich and my dad, Guy Snyder. They lost their dad at a young age but were both able to learn so much from him and ultimately, both were able to make In-N-Out Burger much stronger.'

Lynsi Snyder, President and Owner, In-N-Out Burger

If you happen to wander into the kitchen of an In-N-Out Burger, you will find no freezers, microwaves or heat lamps, no low wages (they start at $10.50 an hour; minimum wage is $7.25), proper healthcare for full-time employees, and paid holidays and sickness benefit. This sounds so alien when talking about a fast-food restaurant, but the result of these excellent working conditions is the positive experience each and every customer has when entering the restaurant. It really matters to the company that the employees are happy, that the food is of a certain quality, and this is reflected in the customers packing the place out.

'Best burgers ever, outside of Big Kahuna in the US. Everything is fresh, not frozen, the kitchen is all open-plan so you can see the process, and they are all family-run restaurants so no chance of them falling behind when taken over by franchises. There is a secret menu and only limited choice so it is all made with care and attention – the employees don't have 50 items to try to remember and get out fast. And skin-on fries :D'

Leighsa Henderson, a satisfied customer

Probably the greatest weapon in In-N-Out Burger's marketing arsenal, and a testament to the company's commitment to doing things differently, is its 'secret menu'. Basically, this allows you to order custom burgers, some at no extra cost, from a menu that is largely kept under wraps. Imagine another fast-food chain having a secret menu: it just wouldn't be possible, what with all the strict brand guidelines, as stated in the brand bible. I'm not sure how you were meant to find out about this menu when it was first introduced, but that doesn't matter now because it's not exactly a secret anymore (the most popular items on the menu can be found on the company's website). Once I'd discovered it, it changed my experience of fast food forever. The 'Animal Style' is the most popular secret item: a regular burger with pickles, extra 'spread' (a sauce similar to

Thousand Island dressing), grilled onions (instead of fresh) and mustard fried on to each patty. A 'Wish Burger' is the veggie option, with no meat or cheese. You can even specify how you want your fries cooked, from well done to no salt to 'Animal Style' (fries topped with melted cheese, grilled onions and spread).

Just thinking about In-N-Out burgers makes me want to go out and grab one ('Flying Dutchman' – two patties, two slices of cheese, no bun, extra everything), but I'd have to jump on a plane: at the time of writing, there were no In-N-Out Burger restaurants in Europe. A few US gourmet-burger chains have opened in the UK – Five Guys Burger and Fries, Shake Shack – and you'll still have to queue up to get into one. In 2012 In-N-Out Burger opened a one-day-only pop-up store in Hendon, north-west London, to test the market, but so far there has been no announcement about when the first restaurant proper will open.

In-N-Out Burger's recipe for success:

1. A real family business
2. Quality and transparency
3. Look after your employees and your customers will feel the benefits
4. The not-so-secret menu

#12
Manufactured Desire

Let's begin with where commerce is right now. And when I say 'commerce' I mean the mass market referred to in the introduction – the high street/retail park/shopping mall businesses, in other words, whether analogue or digital. These are the companies making the kinds of goods that rely on the advertising and marketing industries to get word out there, the idea being that it sticks in the mind of the consumer long enough to result in a sale. This is the old model and it's broken, defunct. Not only because of the glut of virtually identical products out there (which in turn creates a huge digital noise), but also because consuming as much as you can with little regard for anything other than satisfying your material needs is not going to end well, either for humanity or for the planet. The real kicker is that these 'needs' aren't genuine needs at all, like food, heat, shelter or transport, but manufactured desires. In the end, it's all about getting us to consume.

'What this crisis [the financial meltdown of 2008] has taught us is that, at the end of the day, there is no real separation between Main Street and Wall Street.'

Barack Obama

There are five main categories of consumption: food, housing, transportation, consumer goods and services. These are part of what is termed the 'material economy', which, in turn, can be broken down into the following stages:

extraction > production > distribution > consumption > disposal

The problem with the material economy is that it's a linear system being run on a planet with finite resources. Which is a recipe for disaster. As it moves through the above stages it has a negative effect on society, culture, the economy and the environment. It feeds the market with cheap, consumable products, most of which carry 'externalized costs', i.e. the true but usually hidden costs of producing or consuming a good or service, such as the use of cheap/slave labour, the over-extraction of scarce resources (usually from Third World countries) and environmental damage. While carrying out research for her film *The Story of Stuff* (2007), the American sustainability champion Annie Leonard – who we'll be hearing from later – discovered that, of the goods flowing through the US consumer economy, only 1 per cent remains in use six months after purchase. In other words, 99 per cent of the goods sold on Main Street are absolute rubbish.

Writing in 1955, the American economist and retail analyst Victor Lebow set out what many consider to be the blueprint for mass consumption:

Our enormously productive economy demands that we make consumption our way of life, that we convert the buying and use of goods into rituals, that we seek our spiritual satisfactions, our ego satisfactions, in consumption. The measure of social status, of social acceptance, of prestige, is now to be found in our consumptive patterns. The very meaning and significance of our lives today expressed in consumptive terms. The greater the pressures upon the individual to conform to safe and accepted social standards, the more does he tend to express his aspirations and his individuality in terms of what he wears, drives, eats – his home, his car, his pattern of food serving, his hobbies.

These commodities and services must be offered to the consumer with a special urgency. We require not only 'forced draft' consumption, but 'expensive' consumption as well. We need things consumed, burned up, worn out, replaced, and discarded at an ever increasing pace. We need to have people eat, drink, dress, ride, live, with ever more complicated and, therefore, constantly more expensive consumption. The home power tools and the whole 'do-it-yourself' movement are excellent examples of 'expensive' consumption.

By the end of the twentieth century the United States (closely followed by the rest of the world) was well on the way to consuming itself. But this kind of consumption isn't something that happens naturally. It was helped along not only by planned obsolescence, which we've already come across, but also by such models as 'perceived obsolescence', which encourages consumers to throw out something that still works perfectly but appears to be outdated, thanks to its continual redesign – think mobile phones, trainers and laptops. Throw in some hardcore marketing shtick and you're on to a winner (or loser, depending on your point of view).

Now for the good news. The Unbrandables want to look after their world, and are turning their backs on all aspects of the material economy, especially the products it produces. Hopefully the rest of the planet will soon follow suit, but until then the Unbrandables are leading the way in consumer conscience.

#13
A Poem by Tony Kaye

i love everything to do with apple.
i love that they made me think about standing on a stage and
    talking about what it is you do.
i love that they made me think about working harder.
i love that they made me think.
i love that they made me not be a snob anymore.
i love that they showed me that art can be anything and everything.
i love that they defined what a brand was.
i love that we are all apples and not oranges.
i love apple.
i love flying planes and recording machines travelling all over the world.
i love.
i love colour more than i ever loved colour before in my whole life
    because of them and jonathan ive.
i love that i found out it was ok to be difficult if it meant getting
    something done better.
i love that if you wanted to be a magician that could become as
    important as being john lennon.
i love that everything speaks in a language that everyone and no
    one understands.
i love that i can not make sense because it's so much easier than
    making sense.
i love that apple makes my kids more clever.
i love the apple has made my family more clever.
i love the apple has made me more clever.

i love that apple is a brand of band aid paid always to the full
of life said done only better.
i hate that steve jobs had to die, that makes me cry.
i hate every brand that does not try as hard as he did to respect
the consumer with unparalleled integrity.
i don't hate anything because hate is stupid and i am stupid
enough as it is.

#14
Unbrandable People: Tarryn-Lee Lamb Warner

Tarryn-Lee is an anthropologist from Port Elizabeth, South Africa, who actually lives the whole Unbrandable philosophy. Although fiercely Unbrandable, she does still have some loyalties, which is what this journey is all about.

'Buying into brands has never really appealed to me', she explains. 'Although it's impossible to be totally "unbranded" in this day and age, I have never liked that idea of selling the same merch or ideas to millions of people. Brands work for different people in different ways, but they still sell the same product, with the same intention and with the same purpose behind it. Brands in my opinion do not encourage individuality, they smother it.

'I see the whole Unbrandable movement changing the nature of brands completely. We basically live in blur. We are under siege all day, every day. People, ideas, products, slogans, messages. In such a rapidly moving environment, brands have to begin to offer something real, and not only different but intellectually stimulating enough to make us slow down and take notice. I look at so many brands doing the same thing. The same marketing, the same products, the same traps. Brands need to start unbranding themselves. They need to unpack their brands and offer products, services, ideals, messages and concepts to the minority and not the masses.

'To really make a difference in the future, brands will have to have a very lucid and overarching practice of responsibility. Making a difference in any context you look at. Whether it be the integrity of their product, the production and selling of the product, the impact that they have as manufacturers on our natural and social environments – it all requires a sense of responsibility towards the environment in which we exist as producers and consumers. It's the same as being a role model. Your actions inspire and validate those of others.'

#15
Unbranded Brands: Nudie Jeans

Founded in 2001 in Gothenburg, Sweden, Nudie Jeans is a fashion brand with a difference: it actually cares about the planet, human rights, the customer and its products. All this is amply demonstrated by the company's work with Amnesty International, including, in 2007, the creation of a range of T-shirts illustrating the thirty articles of the Universal Declaration of Human Rights. In the fickle world of fashion, this was an Unbrandable step forward. Fashion does care!

Any brand that offers its customers free in-store repairs or the chance to send away for a free repair kit has to be worth checking out. But does this make a difference when it comes to deciding which brand of jeans to buy? It does when the first thing on your checklist is 'Do they give a shit?' Nudie Jeans' online production guide shows the customer exactly where each item is manufactured. The company is also an affiliate of the Fair Wear Foundation, a not-for-profit organization that works closely with the clothing industry to improve employment conditions for garment workers. There is even a Nudie Jeans online forum (mynudies.com), where you can share all your Nudie experiences with fellow Nudie-lovers.

'We love jeans, a passion we share with anyone who mourns a worn-out pair like the passing of a close friend. No fabric ages quite as beautifully as denim; the longer you wear your jeans, the more character and attitude they acquire. You shape them with your lifestyle, and they become like a second skin. Jeans

share the same soul and attitude found in the rock
'n' roll scene – they're both part of the same culture.
Nudie Jeans will always stay true to jeans. We're not
looking for fly-by-night fads; our inspiration is found
far from the world of glamour and catwalks. We don't
just offer jeans. We offer a way of thinking, a concept,
and an undying passion, fuelled by the traditions of
denim and the characteristics of the fabric itself.'

Nudie Jeans mission statement

Why Nudie Jeans works:

1. No hidden costs (for the planet, the customers or the workers)
2. Attention to detail (the consumer knows everything about the product)
3. The best after-service care imaginable

#16
Consumption

'I took a little editing job once, and it was one of the worst things I've ever done in my life. It was all about numbers, traffic and content. I was disillusioned by the way media is going these days. You go to someone and pitch a great idea: you've got the fixer, the contact, I can do it right now. They're like, "That's an amazing idea, but how are you going to get there?" Well, as I'm writing the article for you, you're gonna send me. But they're like, "Sorry, there's no budget for that." It's hard. I knew I was never going to be some desk jockey – it's near pointless writing about a big story without actually being there. At Vice News they understand that, and it's a great place to be right now for a journalist.'

Jake Hanrahan, journalist

When it comes to consumption, Western society has a voracious appetite – not just for products or brands, but also for 'content' and other forms of entertainment. Given the kinds of things that are trending online, it seems that attention spans are shorter than they've ever been. To get the masses to watch a 3-minute video is nigh on impossible; 60 seconds is about the average these days. But this isn't just affecting the world of brand communication; it often appears as though the mainstream media have gone slightly mad, too. Ultimately, these developments will have an knock-on effect on the digital generation's cultural heritage.

In short, if things continue as they are, they won't have one. It will be all blipverts and online features made up of images lifted from elsewhere. This may sound like an exaggeration, but all you have to do is check your social-media feed and see how much of the content you are being redirected to is original.

'Photojournalism has had it. It's all gone celebrity. It's had it. Nobody wants to look at spreads of dying children. They want to see higher heels. It's all gone celebrity, hasn't it? Celebrity, looks, fashion. If I see another picture of Gwyneth Paltrow, I think I'll put my head down the lavatory. Fake tans, Beckhams, Jamie Oliver. I can't take any more of it. That's why I'm going to Syria. I haven't been to Syria for a decade, since the Gulf War started. And I'm going right back to the place where I crossed over the border ten years ago. I ask myself: why am I giving up all this comfort to go and sleep in a derelict house and slosh around the Turkish border with poor old refugees? I just want to keep in touch with myself. I don't want to become complacently comfortable. If I don't keep prodding myself at my age – I'll be seventy-eight at my next birthday – I'm going to get Alzheimer's; I've already had massive heart problems and surgery. You've got to keep in touch with yourself; you've got to remind yourself that there's still something left.'

Don McCullin, photographer

Let's look at this from an Unbrandable perspective. In order to safeguard our cultural heritage, we need to reclaim our culture from the brands and the mainstream media. This is the only way to ensure that what we've created – be it fashion, music, art, food, literature or film – stays true to the cause. First of all, the truly interesting stuff, the genuinely authentic cultural events, happen spontaneously, from the ground up. Nowadays, a lot of people live in an online dream-bubble, reading, watching, buying things off the Internet, or going to branded music festivals and big art shows, all under the illusion that they're part of something real – a movement, perhaps. But what they're doing – and this is the vital point – is confusing consumption with culture. Just because they rock up, pay their money, get their sneaker tagged, buy a T-shirt and listen to some piped-in culture doesn't mean that they've done something culturally significant. They need to create their own culture, to do way more than just read a post or watch a very short video clip. They need to dive into the glorious abyss that is culture and set themselves free …

It's not that we should stop working with brands altogether; most of us can't afford to. Rather, we should also be doing other work that is 100 per cent pure and unadulterated. Whenever I'm on a commercial job, I'm actually writing and shooting ten other ideas off the back of it, perhaps only one or two of which will ever see the light of day. It's this work that is important for our collective cultural heritage. This, in my opinion, is the way forward. The future.

'I had no idea who King Adz was and why I'd been sent a copy of *The Stuff You Can't Buy*, but then I started reading and it reminded me of how totally old I am and how out of the loop I am. But I'm a Luddite, and I think that the digital revolution has destroyed everything I hold sacred – music, movies, books. My agent in New York, third-generation literary agent at an old, established firm – in the 1980s, when I met him, he'd get 400 books a year. He'd read all of them and choose to represent maybe 10 per cent and then do it properly. Now he gets 6,000 manuscripts a year, and reads hardly fucken any of them. Because the means of production have been democratized, anyone can write a book; I'm making a fucken record in my bedroom. All this great liberation they've promised us is fucken empty.

This week in South Africa the biggest record company, which has been going for eighty-seven years, ceased to exist as a company except as an archive. Exclusive Books is up for sale but no one wants to buy it, and it's the last book chain in South Africa. All the traditional TV and movie post-production houses are going under – and leaving us with what? I know what the fuckers who run the Internet want to do: feed us horse shit. We'll have *Pop Idol* winners, celebrity gossip and that's it. And the really rich people are going to get the information, which guys on bikes will deliver in brown paper bags, which will be hammered out on Remingtons. They will know what's going on, and the rest of us will know what's going on in *Idols*.'

Rian Malan, writer

The emergence of television may have threatened to kill the cinema, but the digital revolution has threatened to kill them both. When it comes to entertainment, let alone the way brands are sold, the changes to how we consume are just the tip of the iceberg. In the world of commissioning, for instance, the rules of engagement have changed – thankfully for the better. The fact that other platforms (online catch-up and video-streaming services, etc.) are now commissioning original content is great for the many talented people out there who have been kept down by those TV commissioners who seem to have no vision whatsoever and treat their audiences like morons. The way everything is now consumed has made it easier to get good work out there. As long as it's on a well-hyped platform (YouTube just doesn't cut it anymore, as we shall see in a moment), is original and is promoted properly, it will travel. It will get eyeballs. This, surely, is something that the Unbrandable brands have to tap into.

'We have a particular condition in Brazil. We have one TV station that controls 55 per cent of the audience

and most of the money. We have one press company that controls twenty-five of the top magazines. They do it in a very good way so the money is not spent outside of these channels. Our Internet access is not very fast; actually, it's shit. So the people's experience with the Internet is not what it should be. A viral hit could be 10,000 views, but a good 30-second TV spot in the most popular soap opera, for 450,000 reals [£110,000], can reach 80 million people. We have 200 million people in Brazil. Culturally speaking, television made us as a country, and this is important.'

Celso Loducca, Brazilian advertising legend

When I was promoting the South African edition of *The Stuff You Can't Bottle*, I appeared on the SAfm Media Show. When the interview was over, I tuned into the show on the drive back from the studio and ended up listening to the next guest, a creative director of an old-school ad agency. He had been invited on to the show to talk about his latest TV spot, which he proceeded to describe in minute detail. And it all sounded rather pathetic. The ad was aimed at the youth demographic, and was for liquorice allsorts – a product we all know the youth go crazy for … He spent a good few minutes talking about the 'incredible' client and what a great ad it was. A TV ad. On the radio. The fact that this guy was appearing on a radio show to promote a TV ad aimed at the youth that no one would care about, let alone respond to, said everything I needed to know about the state of the union.

'The 30-second TV ad is dead. Thirty long seconds has become the standard dull unit of consumption. That's boring. Piss or get off the pot. We need to break its monotonous stranglehold. Thirty seconds is a lifetime now. You can (and we all do) skip an ad after 3 seconds on YouTube. In other words, we all know whether

we like something after a couple of seconds. We're absorbing things much faster these days. Let's tell very short stories or huge long ones. Go super short or hugely long. Break the rhythm. Then people will notice. And don't ask why it took me so many words to explain that. I had you at "the 30-second ad is dead".'

Trevor Beattie, adman

'Extreme consumers' is a terrible phrase for people living 'off-grid', many of whom are perceived to be living in the future. It's for this reason that brands examine them so closely, crystal ball-style, to see if there is anything for them to cling on to. This practice is often termed 'co-creation' – the re-branding (i.e. theft) of an existing idea for right here, right now (see #51, 'No One Really Knows Anything', page 154). The strength of such consumers' opinions supposedly shows the brands how far they can push the boundaries of their brand communications, what the limits are. I'm not sure if any of this actually works, however. The problem is that if you take your subject out of its natural habitat, it will invariably behave in a different way. Think about it. It's like focus groups telling the brands what they want to hear.

This leads us to the myth of YouTube. The online video-sharing website was once heralded as the death of mainstream TV, but ten years on it's become a cultural/content black hole that sucks in your creations and then confuses your audience. As a user you can go to the site with one intention (to watch a video or advert that everyone has been talking about) and end up watching a panda playing an electric guitar. And then there are the comments – which I will talk about later. Much later. As a producer you can spend £40,000 on a video and 400 people will watch it. I'm not going to do the maths on that: it's way too depressing.

In May 2009 *Time* magazine named YouTube as one of the ten biggest tech failures of the previous decade, and I can't help agreeing with them. As humans, what we cannot cope with are unmediated, unlimited streams of content. We need editors and programmers and curators (although this last word is extremely overused). What we need, in other words, is decent TV, and this is why we're returning to the power of broadcast. The circle is complete.

Finally, a word on one of the ways in which all this consumption is having a direct effect on our lives, on our behaviour. Increasingly, people are using the digital world – accessed via their smartphones, tablets, laptops, whatever – to replace human interaction. It's not unusual, for example, to hear of families communicating with one another via social media when they're in the same house, even the same room. In fact, it's true of my own family, but in a slightly different way. For one reason or another, we don't spend a lot of time with members of the extended family, and because of this my mother-in-law communicates with my daughter solely through Facebook. ('She "likes" everything I put up', Kaiya told me one night. 'My friends are like, "Who's that 'liking' every photo?" and I tell them, it's just my granny.') Clearly, we need more human interaction, not less – and this is where brands can help out.

#17
Unbrandable People: Chuck

Chuck lives in the wilderness of Oregon. He had a very successful career in architecture before becoming a landlord, and ended up owning a lot of property in Olympia, Washington. Then, however, he decided that his life was a façade. He dropped out, built a log cabin on a plot of land he owned, high up in a conservation area, and has almost become a recluse. He has a diesel generator and a solar-powered water-heater. The winters are quite tough, he tells me, but not bad enough to make him return to civilization. His dogs keep him company, and he flatly refuses to have his photo taken or to be directly quoted in this book: he has, he says, dropped out for a reason. The one luxury he allows himself is a Kindle. He charges it in his pickup truck and gets his daughter – a friend of mine – to download books for him. There was nothing branded in his cabin except for this one electronic device. Chuck really loves his Kindle, and enjoys nothing more than lighting up a big fat spliff (he grows his own marijuana in the summer) and diving into a classic book, his trusty hounds by his side. Life of Riley, if you ask me.

#18
Unbranded Brands: John Altman

One of the slacker-est, most Unbrandable ideas out there is the
John Altman brand (and I use this word in the loosest sense of the term).
On first sight it's a brand seemingly steeped in American counter-culture,
but in actuality it comes straight out of Amsterdam. John Altman (not
to be confused with the English actor who played Nick Cotton in BBC
TV's *EastEnders*) was an all-round American dude who baked the most
delicious cookies and sold them on Baker Beach, San Francisco – wearing
nothing but an apron and some flip-flops. As a brand, John Altman is
an interesting, intriguing mix of myth, social experiment, independent
thinking and a good old slice of hippy attitude, all wrapped up in the
taglines '100% good, not perfect' and 'Spread the Love'.

**'John Altman is not guilty. He enjoys the good things
in life without the guilt trip that a lot of people impose
on themselves. And he's not guilty because he is
honest, and cares about other people and the planet.'**

John Altman brand statement

John Altman the man caught the imagination of two Dutch admen –
Onno and Hajo – after they bumped into him on the beach one day. They
bought one of his cookies, and decided that they'd never tasted anything
so good. After hanging out with John for a few days, they were entrusted

with the recipe and sent off to spread the word. The public liked what they heard, and now the John Altman brand has branched out from cookies to popcorn to wine to a guide to living well. What more do you need?

'John Altman exists to carry on John's work in his absence and spread the love across the world. We do this by creating things that make the world a better, happier place and have as little impact on the environment as possible. Each month we activate people through our website [johnaltman.org] and our Facebook community to share our pledge of the month to help make the world taste a little sweeter. We like to think that's what John would have wanted.'

Onno Lixenberg and Hajo de Boer, cookie-bakers and admen

The John Altman brand makes a connection because:

1. it's 100 per cent honest;
2. it has a great backstory (who is John? Is he real?);
3. the products are top-notch and made from quality ingredients.

#19
Words with the Shaman: Denzyl Feigelson

As I mentioned earlier, I met Denzyl during a meeting with the Smirnoff Africa bigwigs at the Hurlingham Club in south-west London. I had no idea who he was until afterwards, when I searched for him online. The man behind iTunes. Apple. Say no more. Turn the clock forward and I find myself at Apple's headquarters in Cupertino, California, where I've come to find out Denzyl's thoughts on the Unbrandables.

I start by asking Denzyl about the changing face of consumption – a topic about which I'm always keen to hear other people's opinions. 'I think people have become very non-conscious about consumption', he begins. 'It doesn't really matter if more plastic bottles fill the earth; it doesn't really matter as it's just about people being satisfied. That said, there are a lot of conscious people out there who are trying to do their best to change the planet. But, in general, 90 per cent of the population are fully into unconscious consumption.'

Some seriously uncomfortable truths, there. Denzyl continues to talk about how certain brands, which have become very successful, are into unconscious production. But it's not all bad. Take, for instance, Ben & Jerry's. Having started out from this really hippy-dippy place, the ice-cream brand must have totally freaked out when it realized that it was creating a mountain of empty ice-cream containers on a weekly basis. 'They showed us how to react', says Denzyl. 'It was like, "What are we going to do about this? And this is just us – just one company." The concerned among us worry about landfills and trash and where it all goes, that kind of thing, but I think that there's a lot of unconscious consuming going on.' Will there ever be a shift away from this type of consumption? 'Something horrible has to happen – some catastrophic event has to wake people up. And it does from time to time, but then it rolls back round again. Disney is a great brand because every seven years they have a completely new generation that they can tap into. Disney will always be that brand – and there are other brands like that out there – that will always have an audience to consume them.'

Talk turns to the power of social media. The fact that people's lives are now defined by how much time they devote to the likes of Facebook, Twitter, etc. – and everyone's at it, from young children to pensioners, which is a massive demographic – means it's a powerful force indeed. On the one hand it's a positive thing, helping to connect people, while on the other it's very negative. Almost a culture-killer. 'It's very powerful', agrees Denzyl. 'Very "underground" powerful. I mean, we can turn our noses up at it all we want, but it's driving, it's hard core, and it keeps getting more and more hard core … People are addicted to it – to Instagram, to Pinterest, to Twitter. The book I'd like to write is called "Spiritual Technology". Where is it, the glow in all this social media, in all this technology? Where's the soul in this, and what can we do?'

We return to the subject of brands, and I ask Denzyl what he thinks of the idea that brands are becoming much more sophisticated in their use of digital technology to break into the marketplace. 'The whole ad-agency world is completely upside down right now,' he observes, 'trying to figure out how to break through, how to use social media, online, how to use traditional media, print, radio, television … All these things are up for grabs.' Hearing Denzyl say these words makes me a very happy man. I've been saying the same thing for some time now, and here's Mr iTunes backing me up. After a pause, and with the hustle and bustle of Apple HQ swirling around us, I venture to ask Denzyl which brands he thinks are doing interesting work. 'It's funny,' he replies, 'but I don't really focus on brands. I mean, I like some of the things that catch my attention. British Airways are trying to do some interesting things with these events called UnGrounded – putting a hundred young tech luminaries on a plane and having them solve the world's problems in 12 hours. So there are brands doing good things.'

One branch of the brand family with which Denzyl is familiar is that of shoes – from Puma to Nike to Vans to Converse – as they've all tried, in some way and at some time, to get into music. 'Then you look at the alcohol brands and Red Bull, and at the Coca-Colas and the Fantas and all that kind of stuff, and these are massive corporations and they all struggle with how they feel about their own brands, even though they've been around forever. Still everyday they ask: Who are we as a brand? We have to redefine ourselves, it's new generations now, people aren't buying our products anymore … are we slipping in our market share?' Which, after all, is what it's all about.

On the face of it, Denzyl appears to be Unbrandable, with no labels on show, all clambering for attention. But dig a little deeper and you'll find a different story, albeit one with a very personal element. 'The older you get,' he explains, 'the more you realize that all you have in this world is time, so you go for maximum efficiency. The shoes I have on – they actually have a branded story because they're a combination of John Varvatos and Converse, so they have a bit of style and comfort. The socks I like are Paul Smith, because they stay on my feet. These trousers I got in Italy from a company called Transit, because if you feel them they're amazing …' Even though the branding is subtle, the connection is authentic, part of Denzyl's own backstory.

Considering where I was, and what Denzyl does for a living, I had to ask him about the digital revolution and what influence it's had on the music scene. 'I think it's had a very positive influence', he replies. 'And with a very positive influence comes a backlash over mediocre content. And that's just going to happen, but that's OK because that gives the listener and the consumer the ability to make a choice and differentiate. There's more music being enjoyed and shared and created at this moment in time than at any other in history. Take me – someone who is immersed in music everyday. The most exciting thing in my day is to discover something new, that I then fall in love with. Or to listen to a great album through great speakers, from beginning to end, and go, "What an amazing record!"'

In Unbrandable terms, I think the digital revolution has had a very positive influence on music because (a) it's kicked the industry on its ass, which it needed to be, and (b) it's allowed people to be really creative and to focus on their craft. Even if we're back to a singles-driven market, albums are still selling, and this could be because musicians have been forced to make better albums: there's no room for weaker tracks as they just won't get downloaded. Denzyl appears to agree: 'Record companies are no longer stuck on that old "just give me one or two hits for radio and the rest is filler – I don't care what you make on the rest of your record because we're selling a $20 piece of plastic that people are forced to buy for one or two songs". That's gone, and I think iTunes had a big part in killing that.'

Which is where I came in – iTunes, or rather finding out that Denzyl was pretty much responsible for the whole thing. I ask him about the music industry's reaction to iTunes. Did they see it as a threat? I'm thinking here about the launch of MTV, which the big record labels tried to prevent. 'It's not that iTunes was going to kill the industry,' says Denzyl, 'it's just that they thought it would never work. They were like, "Are you kidding?" Some got it, because they saw the writing on the wall, but it took a lot of work. I've read that about MTV. Unfortunately MTV has been the cause of its own demise because it made some bad decisions. These companies get huge, and they lose sight of their priorities. But when we started out, the industry put up a big wall.'

#20
Unbrandable People: Gili

Not long ago I travelled to Jerusalem to photograph and interview
the city's only skateboarding team. After getting lost a couple of times in
the ancient and winding streets at the heart of the city, I eventually met
up with the team's owner, Gili, a larger-than-life, great bear of a man
with a heart of gold and a hug that nearly broke my back.

In addition to heading up the skate team, Gili is the founder and
owner of Gili's Skateshop, a downtown skating emporium sandwiched
between a travel agent and a Nepalese clothing store. 'I started the
shop as everyone here was being really evil to the skaters', Gili explains.
'I wanted to help them out, mentor them.' After leaving school at the age
of fifteen, Gili ran a stall at a flea market, and discovered skating when it
became popular in the 1980s. Then, after his first (toy) board broke and
he realized that there was nowhere to purchase a replacement, he started
to buy and sell second-hand skate parts and spares.

Opened in 2002, Gili's Skateshop started life in a flat opposite a small
skate park in the suburbs of Jerusalem. At the time, the park was popular
with drug dealers, but Gili cleaned it up and it soon became a hub for
local skaters. When they weren't at school, kids would be dropped off at
Gili's by their parents, as it was safe from suicide bombers. There, they
would hang out in the shop, watch skate videos and skate in the park.
'No bombs ever went off near there', says Gili. Strangely, it was thanks
to the suicide bombers that Gili was able to move the shop to its current
location in the centre of Jerusalem. Because of the large number of
bombs going off at the time, shop prices in the area fell to an all-time low,
and Gili seized the opportunity to open up the shop that still stands today.

'The suicide bombers have really helped me. They helped me open my shop by forcing the prices down and making it affordable for a guy running a skate shop.'

So what does the future hold for Gili and his skaters? 'I've had the shop nine years', he replies. 'I've watched it grow, and in the end there are going to be a few skate parks in Israel. I never give up. I have my riders, and we're gonna make a movie to celebrate the tenth anniversary of the skate shop. If I'm still here after ten years, then I'll be here for another ten for sure.'

#21
Unbranded Brands: Deus Ex Machina

Founded in Australia in 2006, Deus Ex Machina produces hand-built custom motorcycles while holding the belief that 'doing something is more fun than just owning something'. It also has its own range of surfboards, clothing and accessories. It didn't start out, however, with the intention simply to sell stuff; to quote the company's website, it was more about celebrating the 'culture of creativity' that characterizes the custom-motorbike scene. The Deus ex Machina showroom/café/headquarters in Sydney immediately became a shrine to 'run-what-ya-brung' resourcefulness and street-honest industrial art. The fact that you didn't need to own a Deus to join in – as long as you had a bike, or even just an interest in bikes, that was enough – was central to its success. This philosophy of inclusiveness is the polar opposite of the managing director of BlackBerry not being able even to speak the name of rivals Apple – even though their ex-'global creative director' Alicia Keys was spotted with one. The cult of Deus has now spread across the world, with venues (they are way more than stores) in Venice Beach, California, Milan, and two locations in Bali. Ride to die, indeed!

'The Deus philosophy recalls an era before the various pursuits of fun – motorcycling, surfing, skateboarding, whatever – were marketed into fundamentalist factions. All are welcomed under the Deus roof, where there's simply respect for the honesty and enjoyment of the machine. Inclusiveness, authenticity, enthusiasm.

It's a simple and sincere pitch that has winged Deus Ex Machina across the world. Deus Ex Machina says simply there's no "right way" to do individualism, it's all the same juice.'

Deus Ex Machina mission statement

What makes Deus tick:

1. Motorbike honesty
2. Inclusiveness
3. Solid product

#22
Unbrandable People: Josie Long

A rising star on the alternative-comedy circuit and co-founder of Arts Emergency, a project set up to mentor and encourage future arts and humanities students, Josie brings a fresh, Unbrandable blast of positive energy to the tired, mostly male, often bland world of comedy. What does she think of, I wonder, when she hears the word 'brand'?

'I guess a brand tries to give you some kind of ethos behind what they are selling or providing. I tend to be suspicious or frightened and try to avoid them, if I'm honest. I have a pretty unrealistic and puritanical view of the world sometimes; I prefer anything to the commercial world! I like the idea of committing to handpicked cultural things – like curated websites, small record labels, small publishing houses, i.e. people who collect and curate cultural things I'm interested in. I trust the tastes of certain individuals and I'd see that as a brand. I like to follow specific artists. I like non-profit brands, or brands that have a social conscience built into their MO, like Toms Shoes or Howies. I don't really know.'

Is she loyal to any other brands?

'Oh, gosh. I'm not sure beyond indie record labels and certain publishers, like Canongate. I was thinking about brand loyalties I have (like Heinz baked beans or Andrex toilet tissue) and they're pure childhood conditioning. Argh!'

#23
Unbranded Brands: The Pirate Bay

'I had just hoped that these little cameras would make a kind of revolution where you'd say, "Fuck film school – just do it ourselves!" There's a lot of talent and stuff that could be freed by less respect.'

Lars von Trier, film-maker

Launched in Sweden in 2003, the Pirate Bay is a torrent website (one that facilitates file sharing). It is ten times larger than Napster was at its peak, and has even spawned a political party. The first major law suit brought against the three people running it resulted in the handing out of a $6.6 million fine and eight-month prison sentences. The first band of digital pirates to become famous were, of course, the people behind Napster, which operated from 1999 to 2001 as a peer-to-peer file-sharing service with a single goal: to supply free music to those who didn't want to pay for it. Although the Napster crew became the poster boys for the pirate generation, it was not the first file-sharing service to operate across the Internet (think IRC, Hotline and USENET). Because of the speeds available at the time, and the invention of the MP3, music was the main currency of piracy. No one even dared to think about sharing a movie as the compression technology just wasn't in place.

Not long after Napster's rise, the music industry began its campaign against piracy, by trying to convince the public that such behaviour was not only illegal but also anti-social. In 2001 broadband happened.

This was the moment when everything changed for the film, TV, software and music industries. This was when the pirates really took over. By the mid-2000s the Pirate Bay had become the world's largest file-sharing site, with the focus on films – which could now be downloaded in minutes rather than days. It also opened up the possibility of video-on-demand via the Internet. After a highly publicized raid by the police in 2006, which resulted in the website being shut down for three days, the number of Pirate Bay users doubled when it went back on line. Who says crime doesn't pay?

One of the most amazing and unexpected things to come out of hacktivism (the use of technology to promote political ends) is the Pirate Party, a Swedish political organization active in more than forty different countries. The party's backbone is its strong beliefs: civil rights, direct democracy and participation, reform of copyright and patent laws, free sharing of knowledge, political transparency, freedom of information, free education, and universal health care for all. In other words, everything that big business and its powerful political cronies hate. The party was formed on 1 January 2006 by Rickard Falkvinge, and many of its members had previously been involved with Pirate Bay. In the European Parliament elections held in Sweden in 2009, the Pirate Party received 7.1 per cent of the vote, giving it a single seat (which became two following the ratification of the Treaty of Lisbon). The movement quickly spread to Germany, the United Kingdom, France and Austria. In the Icelandic parliamentary election of 2013, the party won three seats with 5.1 per cent of the vote, its biggest victory to date.

Why Pirate Bay works:

1. The masses move in mysterious ways.
2. As the power of the torrent has shown, once word begins to build and the masses get on board, a brand is able to enter the mainstream with a great deal of force behind it.
3. It has a strong and proactive following – as evidenced by the success of the Pirate Party.

#24
It's About Telling Your Story

The power of narrative in the (un)brand(able) message is not to be underestimated. To put it bluntly, people just want to tell their story. More importantly, perhaps, they want to do it themselves, be it through social media or in real life. But what happens when a website begins to monetize its users' content? What happens when your memories, words, thoughts, films and photos are no longer owned by you, but by some IT giant in Cupertino, California? This is something that the Unbrandables reject wholeheartedly – but it also represents an opportunity to make a true connection with them. Allow them total ownership; don't try and colonize the culture; just let it be.

'These businesses want to have a relationship with consumers that ultimately results in a transaction, which benefits them commercially. So how are you going to get money off people? Not just by putting on a glitzy show around the message that you want to say. It is genuinely about a relationship that is community-based. It's more about having a genuine conversation that makes sense. Ideas that are more generous and give back tend to work so much better than the BIG ADVERTISING IDEA communicated through a 30-second TV spot. If people run around saying that they've got a big idea, what they're talking about is that they have a good script. Ideas are much

more valuable when they're generous or giving, as they are far more relevant. It's better to build your own audience than buy your own audience. One is a relationship that you foster and own for a long time, and the other is renting some eyeballs from Rupert Murdoch for 30 seconds that are then gone.'

Malcolm Poynton, Global Chief Creative Officer, Cheil

The future of the whole copyright/ownership issue lies with such organizations and co-operatives as the California-based Creative Commons and other knowledge-sharing not-for-profits. These bodies enable the sharing and use of creativity and knowledge through the development and dissemination of free legal tools, such as easy-to-use copyright licences that provide the public with standardized ways to share and use their creative work, but with certain limitations as chosen by the creator. These licences are not an alternative to copyright, but exist and work alongside it.

Our burning desire to tell the (digital) world our stories is something of a phenomenon. Testament to this is the fact that almost two-thirds of all American teenagers – a serious number of people – have uploaded self-produced content. One way of looking at the growing popularity of social media and other forms of online storytelling is that they're giving a voice to 'ordinary' or 'regular' people, as well as making a valid contribution to popular culture. But there have already been many cases where this user-generated content has been subsumed into a branding exercise. It's inevitable, really, as the stuff that the brands once had to generate – stories, images, films – is now already out there, ripe for the picking. It could be argued that this is a democratic process, but the reality (in most cases) is that it's simply exploitation.

Whether you call it user-generated content, narrative or whatever, it's had a profound effect on how media is produced (or not, in some cases). In May 2013, for example, the *Chicago Sun-Times* made every one of its staff photographers (including a Pulitzer Prize winner) redundant, and gave the remaining journalists training in how to take photos with an iPhone. 'The *Sun-Times* business is changing rapidly,' ran the official explanation, 'and our audiences are consistently seeking more video content with their news.' The professional photographers of this world must have thought it was bad enough when members of the public started buying themselves DSLRs and calling themselves photographers. But journalists taking their own photos?

The sheer number of people not only creating content but also wanting to make a career out of it is having a hugely negative impact on the creative industries. The professional talents out there charge an amount of money commensurate with their skills. But ad agencies, record companies, brands, etc. are no longer willing to pay the going rate as they know that they'll be able to get someone to do it for next to nothing on the promise that it's their 'big break', that it will give them 'exposure'. As a result, the real talents don't get hired and the job goes to someone with a fancy camera who couldn't shoot himself in the foot. Then the poorly taken images have to be Photoshopped by a retoucher, who is probably the only person on the job who's being paid a decent amount – apart from the marketing or ad agency, of course, who will take a sizeable cut of the budget for their 'creative strategy'.

True talent used to rise to the top. Now it has to fight every inch of the way as there is so much content out there clogging up everyone's screens. Combine this with the fact that no one wants to pay for the most important part of the process – creativity – and you've got a really complex equation.

#25
Words with the Shaman: Omaid Hiwaizi

Omaid is one clever bloke. His insights into the strategies used by brands are unique. More importantly, perhaps, they are also ridiculously relevant to the Unbrandable question. I arrange to meet him in London, in a TV-chef-branded restaurant in Spitalfields Market, so that I can pick his brains.

We begin the conversation by trying to define what a brand is, exactly. Start as we mean to go on and all that. 'Put it this way', offers Omaid. 'A brand in its broadest, most powerful sense starts with a point of view on the world and a reason for existing. So, it's not about product, it's not about identity, it's not about tone or communication – it's about something above all of that. But when it's defined correctly, it then defines what is right among all those other things.' To illustrate his point, he chooses a pretty left-field example. 'I think that the English Defence League has a fairly well-defined brand. And I'm saying this as an immigrant, so I'm not a fan of the EDL, but it has a *raison d'être*. Sometimes when you talk to clients from a commercial point of view and you ask them, "Why do you exist?" most of what's in their head is the line of command up to whoever speaks to the shareholders. So in the end they exist to make money for shareholders.'

If this bottom line is visible in the way in which a company operates, it can often be counterproductive. Even the most corporate of organizations now has to think about how it's going to make the world a better place, or at least make a difference – which then informs the brand. 'The phrase I use is "organizing idea"', says Omaid. 'There's a brand essence that usually advertising agencies and brand consultancies put together to define a company's communications in their broadest sense, from identity through to advertising. If you talk "organizing idea", though, it's that, plus all the behaviour, so it then defines all the products. And if you can get that idea in the middle of the brand, the company – then that's when it is most powerful. The origin of the word "brand" was to do with a label, but it's not that anymore.'

My thoughts turn to the inevitable collision between the brand and the Unbrandable worlds. How will the two interact – planned obsolescence vs brands doing good? 'There's a retail paradigm in brands,' observes Omaid, 'which is to do with seasons and upgrades and so on. We're going to start with one colour, then release all the colours, and then we're gonna have special-edition colours, and then we're going to tweak it a bit … And I'm not just talking about phones – I'm talking about clothes, cars, everything. If you sell the same car for five years, people don't talk about it, so you kind of need a reason for them to get excited.' The other side of planned obsolescence, of course, is companies creating products that are designed to fail: electronic goods that fall apart, cheap clothes that you have to replace after just one wash. 'I think brands that operate correctly end up looking like movements', continues Omaid. 'And in that sense it's about an idea at the centre, which people can buy into, feel a connection with – an idea that they can be led by or which reflects their beliefs. And then you end up with groups of people who are into it, and one incarnation of that is that they all wear T-shirts with the logo on. But it's also about people behaving in certain ways in accordance with their beliefs.'

Now we're talking: this is the Unbrandable movement in a nutshell. But do Omaid's ideas have enough momentum to break into the mainstream, to connect with the masses? His faith in humanity tells him that at some point people are going to get sick and tired of rubbish goods, and think, I've had enough. 'Having said that,' he says, 'if you look at some of the new digital trends – one is Snapchat [a photo-messaging app where messages are deleted after a user-controlled period of time] – it's almost like an extra take on disposability. And so, in a sense, I wonder whether it's actually going to get worse before it gets better. I mean, I can see that platforms like Snapchat and Vine [a video-sharing service that limits the length of each video to 7 seconds], which are all about more distilled content, more blipverts, less substance, are highly attractive. And so maybe what we'll find is that this becomes a kind of level, and that people will still find ways of inculcating ideas, just using different cultural or communication structures.' In other words, it's all about people getting creative with 140 characters or less.

Omaid mentions a piece of research he's interested in. Conducted by Professor Robin Dunbar of Oxford University, it basically says that the more personal the style of communication – think face-to-face conversation, Skype – the greater the satisfaction felt by those involved. Brands, of course, often use quite impersonal forms of communication, so is this going to affect the way in which they engage with their audiences? 'I guess it's all to do with the notion of what engagement is. It will vary from brand to brand and movement to movement, but depending on what they're doing, what they're there for and what they sell, then there'll be different kinds of engagement. I think a lot of value will be driven by tighter two-way engagement, but there's a whole piece of work to do on what the models might be, and on how they might relate to sales. One thing to remember is that the reason why TV is in the position it's in is that chief marketing officers and marketing directors have a devout belief in the mantra "I'll spend this on television and I'll get this per cent market-share increase". And that's not like a hypothesis to them, that's the reality of their life. Until there are similar realities about spending money in digital, social, engagement programmes, then it isn't going to change.'

The conversation goes a bit Philip K. Dick at this point, and we start chatting about the interface between humans and technology. In 2012 Omaid gave a presentation at Digital Shoreditch – an annual celebration of east London's digital entrepreneurs – called 'Is there a Terminal Velocity for Youth and Digital?'. The presentation questioned the rate at which young people are being shaped by technology, and whether or not technology itself is a force for good. While it's clear from the data that some people are more engaged with technology than others, there are too many unknowns to be sure where it's all heading. Just think about the huge technological advances that have occurred in the last thirty years, and then try to predict what might come next. Wearable computers? Devices that can read our thoughts? According to Omaid, the latter may not be that far off, with researchers at the University of California, Berkeley, using the latest brain-imaging technology and computational models to reconstruct on screen what people are seeing in their heads.

It won't be too long before someone invents a device that connects to your head, and all of a sudden you won't need to talk anymore: all you'll have to do to make something happen is think about it. But how long would it be before we lost the ability to speak at all? This is the 'Google effect', where the increasing reliance on technology is having a direct and measurable effect on the make-up of the brain, especially the parts that deal with memory. And these evolutionary changes have happened in a very short space of time, not over millions of years. 'I think that the way things are going to change is bewildering, frankly', observes Omaid. 'It's these devices and the data they collect and how that data is used. In that sense, I guess it depends on the narrative in people's minds and the life story and the things that they do as they live their lives. So what is the role of people in that? What is the role of products, of ideas, of commercial brands? I think that, sooner or later, there will be no way in except on the basis of shared ideals.'

And with these words bouncing around my head, I wave for the bill, salute Omaid and bowl out into the very branded space that Spitalfields Market has become, looking for the rise of the robots.

#26
Unbranded Brands: Shakespeare and Company

A bookshop in Paris where writers can work, sleep and give readings to the public may sound like the stuff of fiction, but it's not. Shakespeare and Company is a unique institution, a place that, despite being featured in Richard Linklater's *Before Sunset* (2004) and Woody Allen's *Midnight in Paris* (2011), has been a well-kept secret for many years. Its very dedicated and very loyal patrons don't want it spoilt by tourists, and who can blame them? The one thing that would almost certainly ruin this literary oasis is masses of people more interested in the hype than in the reality.

The original Shakespeare and Company was opened by Sylvia Beach in 1919, and was frequented by the likes of Jean Rhys, Ezra Pound, Ford Maddox Ford, Ernest Hemmingway and James Joyce. It closed in the early years of the Second World War and never re-opened. The present shop was opened by George Whitman in 1951 as Le Mistral, but was renamed in 1964 in honour of the original. Allen Ginsberg, William S. Burroughs, Henry Miller, Anaïs Nin and Richard Wright have all hung out there. Today, there are thirteen beds at the shop, and it's believed that more than 40,000 writers have slept there over the years. This is Unbrandable stuff indeed. Where do I sign up?

'I don't consider Shakespeare and Company like a brand – maybe that's the secret! The bookshop is a place (we wouldn't consider opening other branches),

an ideal (we try and work with the very clear philosophies put in place by first Sylvia Beach and secondly George Whitman) and it has a very particular energy placing the values of community before the values of money. The way we connect with people is by organizing readings, literary festivals, tea parties, housing writers and artists (all these are free), and organizing a literary prize for unpublished authors.'

Sylvia Whitman (daughter of George), proprietor

Why Shakespeare and Company is still going strong:

1 It is about the art and not the commerce.
2 It is truly unique, in every sense of the word.
3 The owner of the 'brand' understands implicitly why it works – and isn't tempted to expand or exploit it.

#27
Unbrandable Places: São Paulo

In 2006 São Paulo became one of the world's first Unbrandable cities when all outdoor advertising was banned. Walking around the city and not being bombarded by billboards and posters – or visual pollution, as some people call them – is a very strange experience. There are no adverts on the sides of buses or taxis, no outdoor video screens, no storefront branding, no one handing out flyers in public places. It is, in fact, a little bit like going back in time. The man responsible for this state of affairs is Gilberto Kassab, a Brazilian politician who passed the 'clean city law' during his tenure as mayor. At the time of the ban the advertising and branding industries panicked, claiming that the law would result in the loss of 20,000 jobs and hundreds of millions of dollars in revenue – neither of which turned out to be true. If anything, it forced them to be a little more creative. Some eight years on and the inhabitants of the city – the fourth largest in the world – are feasting their eyes on the abundant street and urban art that adorns its unique architecture, while the brands are still finding ways to get their messages into the public realm.

'From the mayor's standpoint the city now has the opportunity of reinventing itself, and I must confess that his daring has brought good results, especially for not differentiating between small commerce and big corporations. Brands known by their strong visual impact and by the fortunes spent on advertising, such as McDonald's, Coca-Cola, Citibank, Starbucks,

etc., had to adjust themselves to the new law ... We have been through streets full of stores without any indication whatsoever of the kind of commerce that went on in there. At this moment only the residents from the neighbourhood recognize the stores, just from habit. The mayor's inspiration comes from the Spanish city of Barcelona, but it is always worth remembering that inside São Paulo there are many countries.'

William Baglione, artist and resident of São Paulo

#28
Unbrandable People: Alan Cooper

Born in 1991, Alan grew up in Luton – a place that, a couple of years ago, he would have referred to as 'shit'. Today, however, he'd probably say that it's actually all right. 'I didn't have the best childhood', he explains. 'There was a lot of stuff that happened that affected me while I was growing up. I didn't realize it until now, but it affected my school life, my friendships, and even though most of the problems had originated through family, it affected that as well. I had to grow up quick where I lived, and from the age of sixteen I was living independently in a hostel.' He's none too proud of some of the things he got up to when he was younger, but that's all part of growing up, if you ask me.

I met Alan, a Young Ambassador for the Prince's Trust, at a youth-marketing seminar. He was on a panel I was chairing, and the story he told about the day his mobile phone stopped working made me sit up and take notice. 'When my phone broke I could focus on what I needed to without being distracted. It showed me how dependent I and others had become on their phones and technology. Don't get me wrong; there are some great things that have come from technology, but easier face-to-face communication isn't one of them. We have lost the personal touch, instead sending emails and browsing websites with our device on our laps. This was the best week of my life. I reconnected with myself, I took in my surroundings and at times it felt like I was in the matrix. Now every day I make a conscious effort to have time out, away from my phone, to allow me to focus on myself.'

Alan's story provides a genuine insight into the lives of twenty-somethings, as most marketing and brand managers assume that the youth are constantly on their mobile devices. When the panel was over, I started talking to Alan about growing up with brands. 'I think global brands can be poisonous,' he began, 'and it's only now that I can truly see this. When I look back to my school days, people were obsessed with what trainers you had on, or which clothes you were wearing. As kids, if we drew a self-portrait we would all incorporate the Nike or Adidas logo into our clothes, even if it wasn't true! This continued into high-school days as well, and I remember it got silly, with people checking the bottom of your football boots just to see if it had the Nike logo on the studs, just to prove they was real. Then it can affect the parents, when the kids are pressuring them to get the most expensive brands just so they can "fit in" around school. If they don't earn enough money, it's hard to provide for what their child wants. But as long as they're fulfilling the basic needs, like a house, food and clothes, does it really matter?'

#29
The Art of Selling and Buying

'Anything that's good commerce will be borne of understanding culture, and anything that's good in terms of a brand cultural connection will come out of commerce … I absolutely agree that there is no point in just coming at it from a commercial perspective, because it all goes back to understanding people, as the nuances and peculiarities around people and culture are much richer than a business model. Often these theories are just validated by some facts, but it's not particularly revealing coming at it from an analyst's point of view. A social-commerce example of this is that the huge global brands, such as Proctor & Gamble, are now selling millions of dollars' worth of products through Facebook. Which actually proves the point that if it's in the place where the people are and becomes part of the conversation, then it becomes commerce a lot easier than forcing it on people. If you don't involve the audience, then brands just try and promote their way out of it.'

Malcolm Poynton

The role of the brand has well and truly changed, from that of creator to that of curator – a point worth remembering in an Unbrandable world.

But thanks to the customer making choices driven by price, not taste, the art of shopping has been corrupted by price points and the relentless BOGOF ('buy one, get one free') marketing bullshit. Have we really been conditioned into wanting two cheap (and probably slightly nasty) things for a fiver, rather than something decent for nine quid? And I'm not just talking about chickens here. In the world of fashion, Primark – or 'Primarni', as it is jokingly known – is a great example. Even if you can brave the horrendous bun-fight on the shop floor, whatever you end up buying will be unwearable within a month, or even after just one wash. You get what you pay for. End of story.

'In our case most of the time it's about looking at what the industry is doing for a product/brand and doing the polar opposite. But then we look at what *we're* thinking at this point in time, 'cause we are the audience too. I would say it's like looking at what the norm is and running in the other direction. Take a Concorde to the other side of the planet. I also believe that lies, the smoke and mirrors, are good things to avoid. Truth and Justice. There is so much content to take in, and one needs to approach it with morals and integrity. Before, we used to sell things based on quality; now we sell things based on price. We hope to change this bit by bit. Sustainability is the most important problem facing us animals – *Homo sapiens*. The cockroaches will be fine. Mash has been dubbed "artvertisers", which is totally wanky, but in a sense you have to keep your craft adaptable and always look for the creation of something fresh in a world of the BDF (been done before) ... There is an infinity of ideas out there, you just haven't thought of it yet. I also like hearing "It's been done before, but not by you".'

James Brown, Mash Design

The way physical products are sold has also changed, from online shopping to peer-to-peer recycling (eBay) to pop-up stores – all of which are new and inventive ways of selling. As we've seen in other contexts, the old model isn't working very well: cut to shot of half-empty high street, a direct consequence of the monopoly of the supermarkets and the way they put the squeeze on not only the independent shops but also the suppliers. But there is a flip side: cut to shot of thriving specialist store offering a unique, personal touch and passion and knowledge about whatever it's selling, things that are completely missing from the hypermarkets and the digital shelves. This, then, is one of the Unbrandable solutions to the dominance of the chains: a small independent shop that survives against the odds because it cares about what it sells and the culture in which it exists. And this leads us to something that the big chains just don't have: authenticity. Cut to the story about the anger directed at the Harris + Hoole coffee chain, which presented itself as a family-owned, artisanal affair, but which actually turned out to be 49 per cent owned by Tesco.

Another Unbrandable answer to the high-street chains is the pop-up store. It's a great idea: someone creative taking over an unused space for a short while and turning it into a gallery/shop/showroom happening. An excellent example of the phenomenon was the Patta pop-up store that appeared in central London in October 2013. For four days that month, the Dutch streetwear brand opened a pop-up version of its Amsterdam store in a disused shop on Monmouth Street, near Covent Garden. Patta, to which we'll return later in the book, is Unbrandable because it has such a strong ethic and such a loyal following.

'I guess every brand/store has its own reason for doing a pop-up. Our main reason was that it's a good way to connect with the people outside your normal surroundings. What type of people are they? How do they perceive the brand? What do they like and what don't they like? It also works the other way: customers can meet the people who work for or with the brand and feel the vibe. It's a good social thing ... and the

whole London experience gave us a lot of energy to keep going and keep walking the path we've been walking. People came out and showed loved. We gave all that love back, so as a whole it was beautiful thing.'

Gee, co-founder, Patta

These days, the ultimate display of brand loyalty is actually to buy something, be it music or film or art. In the olden days we had no choice, apart from making tapes of albums or getting jiggy with a Xerox machine. I'm surprised that so many people still spend money on something that they could download for free from the Internet. On the other hand, it's a sign of hope: a healthy and balanced society must include paid-for culture, as it has to support its artists. But it says a great deal about consumer culture when we have to ask the question, do I rate this product enough to buy it? Obviously, with a lot of products you have no choice – you can't download a bottle of Smirnoff, for example, or leech a COS tank top – but you know what I mean.

Many people's buying habits are of course conditioned by those of others. In 2013 I was asked by Voxburner, a Web-based outfit providing insights into the lives of young consumers, to write an op-ed piece for its annual report *Youth 100*, a list of the UK's top brands as chosen by a selection of the country's eighteen- to twenty-four-year-olds. The list contains many of the brands you'd expect to find in such a report: Smirnoff is the alcohol brand of choice, preferably drunk in a Wetherspoon's, with Coke, while wearing a pair of Converse bought from Amazon using PayPal, probably after watching an ad on YouTube on some kind of Sony-made phone or laptop, just before eating a Domino's pizza with Ben & Jerry's for dessert, possibly while wearing cosmetics or aftershave from Boots. All spot-on data reflecting contemporary tastes and a lot of peer-group influence. In other words, nothing that is going to set the brand-insight world on fire.

Then it came to the section that I'd been asked to write about: the top fifteen grocery brands. The results were as follows:

①	Heinz Beanz	73%
②	Hovis	73%
③	Coco Pops	68%
④	Warburtons	67%
⑤	Kingsmill	67%
⑥	Andrex	61%
⑦	Cathedral City	60%
⑧	McCain	60%
⑨	Uncle Ben's	55%
⑩	Special K	53%
⑪	Birds Eye	49%
⑫	Hellman's	48%
⑬	Lurpack	47%
⑭	Goodfella's	47%
⑮	Jelly Belly	40%

Note: The percentages given above represent the proportion of 1,000 18- to 24-year-olds who, when asked to rate 250 brands, responded as either 'loving' or 'liking' them. The other possible responses were 'no feeling', 'dislike' and 'hate'.

At first glance the results suggest that, when it comes to eating, nostalgia is rampant among the youth of today. Comfort-eating in uncertain times, perhaps? But is this really how their tastes are defined? Does it really all come down to what you were given to eat as a child? I have to admit that I was a bit disappointed when I was given this section to review, but that feeling soon disappeared. The data not only presented me with something new to write about (fresh is always good), but also gave me the opportunity to think about youth consumption in a different light – not in the usual media-speak, but in real terms. Nom nom nom.

Most surprising of all, perhaps, is how pedestrian the choices are: is Heinz really the grocery brand of choice for Generation Me? I'd have expected them to be far more experimental than this. Putting to one side this apparent lack of imagination, there is pretty much no correlation with the brands' marketing activity. Which leads us to ask, how effective *is* the advertising of groceries? Think of a Hovis ad and you'll be taken back in time to that boy on a bicycle; it's the same with Coco Pops and the singing monkey. Andrex? That annoyingly cute dog. Nothing new, nothing fresh created in the last decade or so comes to mind, and certainly nothing that targets our eighteen- to twenty-four-year-old demographic. Where, then, is the ad-spend going? Most of it is directed at sustaining market share, which is the worst kind of advertising because it's all about mindless repetition and, at best, nostalgia. The only remotely interesting brand in the results is Uncle Ben's, which is, I imagine, down to the company's decision to reposition itself as a snack food. It's also an indicator of how grocery brands are having to diversify.

'There are times when interrupting makes sense. But in my experience, it's far less than many like to claim. Rather than interrupting or disrupting ... I think brands actually build some sort of relationship when they're about being meaningful and distinctive. If you embrace interruption, I could argue you are allowing your competitors to dictate who you are and what you're doing ... but if you are true to your values and find ways to use that to empower, enable or engage your audience's wants/needs (rather than what you want them to need), you stand a chance to add something to their life rather than take something away.'

Rob Campbell, strategist

#30
Words with the Shaman: Joey Elgersma

A lover of all things 'street', Joey Elgersma has followed a very interesting career path, working in fashion, styling, film and video. Until recently, he was the marketing director for Bread & Butter Berlin, one of the world's largest trade fairs dedicated to streetwear. I've spent a fair bit of time with Joey, in both Africa and Europe, where we've run workshops together for talented youngsters who can't afford to go to college. What's become clear since our first meeting is that, when it comes to how brands should behave, Joey is definitely one of the good guys.

I meet Joey at Templehof, the enormous, disused Berlin airport that has been the venue for the biannual Bread & Butter since 2009. Immediately, I start to bang on about people reacting against global brands and mass consumption; about how they no longer want to be a part of something that the rest of the world is part of. Pausing for a moment I look at Joey, and despite the fact that he's dressed from head to toe in brands (a crime of which I am also guilty), the man I see is a glorious example of someone who's attitude is Unbrandable. Does he agree with this assessment?

'I always wanted to be Unbrandable,' he replies, 'but I don't know if that can ever happen because I like too many brands, or at least I don't want to give myself exclusively to one brand – which would mean that I wouldn't be available for another brand. In general I'm a consumer, so if I go to the supermarket I try to buy the best products out there because I want the best for myself. Of course it's all about the marketing.'

Subliminal or blatant, marketing is always there. But how do you connect with the large number of people whose tastes are informed by price? By and large, it's possible to divide consumers into two groups: those who are driven by quality (the purists, the lone rangers), and those who are motivated by price (most of us). And the younger the consumer generation becomes, the more it is driven by a 'fast-food' mentality, especially in the brand market. 'These days,' observes Joey, 'kids are no longer interested in buying a pair a jeans that costs $250. They want to go to the high street and buy a shirt or a pair of trousers for 20 or 30 euros because it looks good and it makes them look like Rihanna or Chris Brown. I look at that market, and I see that it's fucking up a lot of things. It's fucking up a lot of independent retailers, which are also brands. No matter which city you're in, if you look at the cool, purist retailers – the ones that buy in goods that they really like, that they want to represent – and next door you have an Other Stories or a COS or whatever, there's always a shit load more people inside the mass-market store. This is something that we cannot fight anymore.'

So are such stores actually brands, or are they simply chains that are endangering the rest of the market? 'I see them as Ikea', says Joey. 'If I buy something from Ikea, after two or three months I hate it. That's also true with the clothes on this level. The masses buy them because they're so cheap and they can wear them for a couple of nights and then they're done; they don't wear them anymore. But it's still 20, 30 euros.'

Part of the problem is that there's no real philosophy behind high-street fashion. It's all about the brands looking around to see what's working elsewhere, at what the market likes and – more importantly – wants. Instead of being born out of a real, authentic culture, fashion 'products' are being created out of a chaotic, psychotic equation: now we want this, we saw that, we want to combine it with these. There's no schedule: most mainstream fashion brands are free-styling at the moment and doing whatever they think will be most profitable. And the sad thing is that, as long as you have a following that is driven by price, it's a model that works. But do the brands have this following because they're cheap? Or are people genuinely loyal to places like Primark?

'Not to Primark,' says Joey, 'but they are to Forever 21 ... H&M has opened up daughter companies for every target group, and so it doesn't matter whether you love the Scandinavian, Berlin-ish look, the LA look or the more grown-up, London-ish look. They cater to all tastes. And at a speed that many other brands cannot keep up with.' This is a major Unbrandable point of interest. The smaller, independent brands simply cannot produce goods as quickly as their high-street counterparts. But this is where they have to think on their feet in order to outwit the mainstream giants. React differently. Come from a place of pure culture, rather than a margin on a balance sheet. Come correct. Do it because you live, breath, eat, sleep fashion (or whatever it is you are producing).

We start to talk about Unbrandable brands, the ones we think are doing interesting things. As always I mention my love for Stüssy, and this leads us on to the subject of Vans. 'I will always love Vans', says Joey, 'because I think it's one of the few brands that really takes care of the consumer. They don't step away from who they are, although I'm not really a big fan of the mother company [VF Corporation]. But still, there are some people there that truly understand. So for me, the people who work at the company behind the brand make it what it is.'

So how do you create a brand that matters? I end the interview by asking Joey if he can identify the key elements of an Unbrandable brand. 'To become an understandable brand', he responds, 'you need to specialize in one thing: it needs to be easily definable. I like too many things, I like to do too many things, to start one brand. It's an undefinable world to me. But if I were going to start a brand, it would probably be something that is completely different. I don't know, it's difficult to say because I need to choose and I don't know what to choose. I need to narrow it down and that has been my problem my whole life … So if I were to start a brand it would probably be a brand to explain what thinking differently really means.'

And off we wander into the Berlin afternoon, surrounded by the world's greatest clothing brands, and what seems like a million people worshiping them.

#31
Unbrandable Places: Spuistraat, Amsterdam

Amsterdam has always been an Unbrandable place, and within the city there is a pocket of even fiercer resistance: Spuistraat, once home to some legendary squats. At the southern end of this busy commercial street is the Spui, a public square renowned for its nearby bookshops and weekly book market. It is also home to a small statue, *Het Lieverdje* (The Darling), a gift to the city from the cigarette manufacturer Peter Stuyvesant. In the 1960s the statue was the focus of anti-tobacco protests and other counter-culture happenings, which gradually migrated into Spuistraat; soon, a large proportion of the street had been turned into squats. Today there is only one squat left on the street, but it is full of art galleries and culture – a hangover, perhaps, from what came before.

'Near Dam Square is the empty NRC newspaper building, squatted in the late 1970s by punks, among them the graffiti legend Dr Rat. There was first an underground gallery, Amok, run by Peter Giele, and later the punk club No Name, where Nina Hagen was a frequent visitor. Later, on the Spuistraat side, there was an underground expo place called Aorta, with many art and music manifestations. Because of the coronation of Queen Beatrix [in 1980], there were many provocative happenings, and the municipality bought the building to ease the tension. Now it is all normal and legalized, with shops and pubs. In the Spuistraat is only one squatted house, Vrankrijk, and that is the one and only punk centre with politically correct and straight-edged rebels. The building was bought by the squatters with the help of some alternative bank.'

Hugo Kaagman, artist

#32
Unbranded Brands: Muji

Muji is a Japanese retail company selling a range of household and consumer goods. It is distinguished from its many competitors by its minimalist aesthetic, its emphasis on recycling, its avoidance of waste (at both the production and the packaging stages) and its strict 'no logo' or 'no brand' policy. In April 2001 the company launched the Muji Car 1000, a badge-less and almost featureless version of the Nissan Micra limited to a 1,000 units. Sold via the company's website, the spartanly equipped car – there was no radio, while the rear seats were upholstered in vinyl – came in only one colour: white. As far as you can get from most new cars, in other words.

Why the Muji Car 1000 worked:

1. The message was all about the anti-car car.
2. It was the polar opposite to a fully loaded SUV, so very eco-friendly.
3. Less is more.

#33
Advertising 3.0: Content Still Rules, OK!

'When we talk about the future of advertising, what we're really talking about is the future of the way people think, the future of ideas. That's what's important. The whole media landscape has changed, and the relevant thing is the strength of good ideas; the ideas are now the selling point, more than any kind of medium. A great media-independent idea is the strongest of all, and will always survive the trends and topics.'

Erik Kessels, creative director

There is little doubt that mainstream advertising has lost its way. It used to be big and clever and funny and thought-provoking. The good stuff was an accepted part of modern entertainment, the topic of conversations with friends. But not any more. In fact, it's fair to say that the traditional model of advertising is well and truly broken. Kaput. The signs were there for all to see, from moronic opera singers and annoying comics-turned-salesmen to fake dentists in shopping centres telling people which toothpaste they should use – it was all so wrong. Did advertisers think that the public were morons? Did they really believe that they'd swallow the blatant lies?

The death of traditional advertising couldn't have come at a better time, and it's all thanks to the digital revolution. The World 2.0 is so savvy and connected and switched on that traditional advertising – print and TV – had to fall sooner or later. Gone, too, is the old empire of 'buy this'. The new regime is all about open, honest communication that begins with the producers finding out what the public really wants. This may sound strange to some of you out there, but it's no longer a case of 'looking out', at where to aim the communications. With digital content, you have to start by 'looking in' – to the very souls of your audience, the people who will be parting with their hard-earned cash. It's the only way forward. If you don't start as you mean to go on, then your work will be just another wasted piece of 'marketing'.

'So think about this: a few years ago there was no Twitter – who could have anticipated something like that? No one has the slightest clue about what the world is going to look like six months from now, let alone six years. But we still have to sell the merch, to communicate, to get people to see the work. And that's where it gets complicated, because it's more difficult than ever to actually communicate as we live in this environment of unprecedented clutter, which is incredibly difficult to cut through. But that's also what makes it so exciting: this is the golden age of creativity.'

Andrew Essex, Vice Chairman, Dro5a

If there's one word that's being abused at the moment, it's 'content'. Everyone in the industry (and out of it, for that matter) knows that content is king; but a lot of people still don't really understand what it means, let alone how to create it properly. When one of the leading photographic agents on the planet asked me what it meant, this is what I told her: 'It's just like advertising, but without thirty-odd people looking over your shoulder – who pretty soon will need some sushi and energy drinks – with a tenth of the budget and no time at all to create the work. But it is still the most exciting and creative part of the business to be in right now.' A few days later, when ad legend Tony Kaye asked me the same question, I knew things had shifted. The bottom line is that content is the conduit between brand and audience, and to understand what makes authentic content work, you have to begin with street culture.

'Street culture is a generation of voices that are trying to express themselves and be heard, but they haven't yet found a proper audience within the mainstream. So they go outside into the world and on to the street and they shout – either literally, or by painting a picture on a wall, or by standing on a corner with a guitar or some form of musical instrument and playing a song, or by doing an open mike session or whatever – and they go through a number of hours, days, weeks, years and ply their craft and try to get their expression out into the world.'

Tony Kaye, director and ex-adman

It's no coincidence that the content that's really connecting brands and audiences is being produced as a by-product of street culture, of exciting, interesting and weird-and-wonderful events happening on or near the street. It has to be. It can't be the usual brand exercise where something is written, story-boarded, focus-tested, rinsed, hung out to dry and then packaged up with a logo at the end and chucked out into the world. It has to be created in an authentic way. Nurtured.

The flipside to this is that there is a lot of inauthentic content out there, which just clogs up the system and makes it harder for the real stuff to break through. And there is definitely a 'real' and a 'fake'. Real is when a nineteen-year-old street-style hustler from Nairobi captures a moment of his or her life and then posts it online – that's the stuff you can't bottle.

Fake is when the likes of Facebook tries to feed you 'trending' articles that are just so irrelevant, irreverent and annoyingly out of touch with what is actually going on in your life. You'd think that, with all this technology, they'd be able to aim that shit a bit better. But this is where it all falls down.

Street culture is not something you can predict or track or analyse using an algorithm. It's a fluid movement, a mix of cultural DNA, style, art, instinct and passion. This is what makes understanding it so much more complex than mining data from a gazillion online posts and hoping to get some live market insights.

#34
Unbrandable People: Douglas Tompkins

'Capitalism doesn't function when it starts to contract, and we can see that quite clearly right here in the Eurozone. It's like pushing a giant monster underwater that's gasping for air. It goes nuts. Capitalism may have all sorts of things that are good, but ultimately it's bad for everyone.'

Douglas Tompkins, environmentalist and entrepreneur

Since selling up and leaving the business world in 1989, Mr Tompkins, co-founder of the North Face and Esprit, has dedicated himself to environmental activism and land conservation. Together with his wife, Kristine (herself the former CEO of outdoor fashion brand Patagonia), he has helped conserve more than 8,000 square kilometres (3,000 square miles) of wilderness in Chile and Argentina, more than any other private individual. He believes that we've all been spellbound by technology – by our phones, our laptops, etc. – and that we are overlooking its true cost.

'We have been poor on doing the systemic analysis, especially in the area of technology criticism. Until we get better at that, I think we're cooked. We're

going to continue to extinct species and we're going to continue to dig the hole deeper of the whole eco-social crisis. If you just hold your mobile phone for thirty seconds and think backwards through its production, you have the entire techno-industrial culture wrapped up there. You can't have that device without everything that goes with it. You see mining, transportation, manufacturing, computers, high-speed communications, satellite communications. It's all there, you see, and it's that techno-industrial culture that's destroying the world.'

Douglas Tompkins

Douglas and Kristine have also made a stand against some of the bigger environmental organizations, such as the World Wildlife Fund and Greenpeace, claiming that they have grown too close to the corporations they should be fighting, are too expensive to run and actually get little done, leaving the real work to the smaller, more nimble non-governmental organizations (NGOs). This is a brave and Unbrandable position to take.

#35
Unbranded Brands: Patta

'It's hard for me to say what makes the brand so real ... I guess it's for other people to say whether this is the case or not. All I can say from our end is that we put a lot of time, effort and ultimately love into everything we do. It's a genuine team effort from everybody involved with Patta, and the close circle of people we like to call our friends. Team Patta 4 real!'

Gee, co-founder, Patta

Part shop, part fashion label and part lifestyle, Patta is indeed the real thing because it comes from such a pure and strong place. It was established in 2004 by a group of Dutch guys from diverse cultural backgrounds who wanted to share their love of sneakers, fashion and street culture. The Patta crew consists of Gee, Edson, Milanello, Danny, Vinz, Masta Lee, Virgil, Thijs, Eben and Idje. Although the design and manufacture of clothes and sneakers forms a large part of what they do, Patta is so much more than that. It's about the ever-changing culture that surrounds the core members. I've been lucky enough to witness at first hand their love of this culture and the strength of their beliefs, and I have the utmost respect for each and every one of them – matched only by my feelings for Stüssy.

At the heart of Patta is the concept of multiculturalism, of immigrants mixing with and enriching the local way of life. Both Edson and Gee are from Suriname, a former Dutch colony, and the word 'patta' is of Surinamese origin. A slang term meaning 'sneaker', it has now entered the Dutch vernacular (thanks in part to the large number of Surinamese living in the Netherlands), which is the ultimate accolade for any brand. To truly experience what Patta is all about, you have to visit its shop, located in the heart of Amsterdam between Chinatown and the red-light district. If you're lucky, one or two of the founding members will be working there – which is also something worth noting if you want to understand why the brand works.

'Selling only shoes was never our aim. We wanted to make a platform for like-minded friends and people with all different kinds of skills ... That has always been the backbone of Patta. I guess the involvement of [Dutch artist] Vincent van de Waal took our clothing/ product output to a higher level – his involvement has been crucial in this respect.'

Gee

Why does the Patta brand rock?

1. It taps into the positive aspects of multiculturalism.
2. It's a focused remix of a huge cultural movement (sneakers × fashion × street culture).
3. It is fierce: you do not fuck with Patta.

#36
Emerging Markets

'With regards to social media, I think there is a lot going on in the emerging markets, but I still don't believe that they really have an opinion yet. They're still trying to find it, so when they get a chance, it's about endorsing brands and sharing experiences and sharing positivity ... There's a lot of that, and a lot of knowledge-sharing. It's the equivalent of the street-corner culture. If you were to travel to one of these markets, you'd find a group of kids or young adults on a street corner, and one of them will have just come back from London or somewhere on an internship, and he'll be sharing that story verbatim. It's almost like he's written it down; he's documented it, he's sharing it and everything he's learned, and the others will take it on as their own. That's the power of the street-corner culture – it's people sharing stuff.'

Leroy Tulip, consumer insight specialist

There has never been such a scramble for the emerging markets: BRICS (Brazil, Russia, India, China, South Africa), MINT (Mexico, Indonesia, Nigeria, Turkey) or whatever acronym the economist Jim O'Neill comes up with next. However you define them, the emerging markets have a voracious appetite for global brands, and are extremely important to producers. I was on a flight out of Russia one morning, and just as the doors were about to close, a lady dressed from head to toe in designer gear rushed on to the plane. Her T-shirt read 'Less Is Poor', carefully picked out in diamonds. Having just spent some time in Moscow, I knew she wasn't joking.

The Unbrandable movement has yet to make itself known in these 'new' territories. It's still too early for any real backlash, and the relationship between brand and consumer is much more complicated than in established markets. Take KFC, for example. In the West, no one likes to admit that they've even *been* to a KFC, let alone that they eat there regularly. In many parts of Africa, however, the bargain buckets come in transparent plastic bags, as there is no clearer indication of your superior social status than arriving home with a bucket or two for your family's evening meal. During my research for this book, I discovered that a lot of schoolchildren in Nigeria do their homework in fast-food restaurants. When I asked some of them why, they responded by saying that the light was constant (no power cuts), they were safe places to work (most restaurants are located in malls with security guards) and they were quiet (way too much noise at home to be able to concentrate).

It's important to understand that brands need emerging markets more than emerging markets need brands. Although many of the countries concerned are described as 'developing', they are not the places of misery they are often made out to be – and nor are they crying out for the prosperous West to ride over the horizon like some colonial John Wayne and save them. The attitude towards emerging markets has been wrong for way too long, and now – because of the oil, the market growth, the mobile-phone boom, the appetite for global brands, the rapidly growing middle class – suddenly they are on the carpetbaggers' radar. These countries are often the most culturally interesting spots in the world, and we should act accordingly. Show them some respect and perhaps we'll get some in return. I once received a list of dos and don'ts from a client before doing a job in West Africa. I'd never read anything so moronic or patronizing: 'Don't try and solve all their problems', 'Don't offer a solution', 'Don't eat the street food', 'Don't venture off the beaten path', 'Never drink in illegal bars (shabeens)' … There is nothing I enjoy more than eating street food in Africa and then shooting the breeze over a cold beer with some nice peeps in a shabeen – while telling them how to run their country. OK, so the last bit isn't true, but you get the idea.

The best way to spread the word about your brand is to come correct. Tread carefully. Show some respect to your future customers, their heritage and their country. Be gentle, do some good – and always spread the love.

'Growth is forced on us, willy-nilly, by the custom of measuring wealth in terms of money. This brings about the appearance of spontaneous increase of wealth by compound interest, a sort of abiogenesis impossible with real wealth. It is clear that without an external source of energy, in this case fossil fuels, the growth syndrome would not have become so important.'

Manfred Max-Neef, economist and environmentalist

#37
Unbrandable Places: Freetown, Kigali

As we're on the subject of emerging markets, let's pay a visit to the heart of Africa: Kigali, the capital of Rwanda. It took a walk with a local reggae band through Freetown, a township-like area in the southern part of the city, to open my eyes to a very unique part of the world. All aspects of African street life were on display: children running around or selling boiled eggs, pots of beans bubbling away, shabeens doing a roaring trade (alcohol, like Chinese food, is available everywhere), and the wide availability of cannabis and khat, a local leaf that is chewed (or drunk as an infusion) as a stimulant.

The band were called Jah Doves, and as we walked I struck up a conversation with one of its members, Ras Patrick. 'I live for music', he told me. 'When I don't play music I don't eat, I don't sleep … It's my life. Before the Genocide [in 1994] people from different ethnic groups would play together. After the war it's about how we teach people about love, unity and change; the message we spread with our music is about being together.'

Wandering through Freetown was a great moment in my life. We walked from one end to the other, and, as you might imagine, attracted a small crowd of children as we went. One of them even held my hand for a while, before running off to let her friend smell the strange scent of the *mzungu* (white man). After an aborted attempt to film a barbecue outside a beer shack – these particular locals clearly didn't want to be filmed, and who can blame them? – we continued walking along the narrow path that runs all the way through the township. Past kids playing pool or snooker on a homemade table, and past the most informal market I've ever seen, with everything from fruit and vegetables to household junk laid out on tattered sacks, all ready to be scooped up if and when the police made an appearance. Most significantly, perhaps, there was absolutely no branding on show, and no one in charge but the people themselves. Welcome to Freetown.

Although Nokia as a brand of mobile phone no longer exists (thanks, Microsoft), out in the developing world it is still flying the flag for the Unbrandables. Key to its ongoing visibility there is a booming market for second-hand mobile phones and – unlike in the West, where the smartphone rules the roost – the continued popularity of so-called bricks: outdated, 'obsolete' mobile phones with the most basic of functions. And the poster boy for the brick is, undoubtedly, the Nokia 1100.

In brand-image terms, Nokia was the outcast of the mobile-phone world. As part of my research for this book, I read a report saying that Nokia's survival in such a fiercely contested market may have been down to the fact that, in contrast to its image-obsessed competitors, it represented 'progress with purpose'. One of the hidden problems with the mobile-phone industry is that the technology relies heavily on so-called conflict minerals, natural resources extracted in conflict zones – often in terrible conditions for the workers – and sold to finance the fighting. These minerals are an essential part of all modern mobile phones, and by continuing to turn a blind eye to their origins, the manufacturers appear to be condoning the misery associated with their extraction. Nokia was one of the few global brands that tried to address this problem.

'Of the [mobile phone] manufacturers, Nokia appears to have gone furthest, and its efforts [were] quite impressive ... Long before most other companies

began to take an interest [it tried] to remove illegally mined tantalum from its supply chain. It [instructed] its suppliers to map the routes these metals [took] before they [reached] the company.'

George Monbiot, writer

The 1100 is the model that made Nokia the most used brand of mobile phone on the planet. Basic yet extremely robust, it has a torch function and will float if dropped in water; dry it out and it will continue to work, something that cannot be said of almost every other modern mobile phone. Back in 2011, Nokia had a 58 per cent share of the African mobile-phone market, giving Coke a run for its money in the brand-recognition stakes. The 1100 is no longer in production, but that hasn't made much difference to its key markets, where for many people the only affordable way of owning a mobile phone is to buy one second-hand.

What was the secret of Nokia's success?

❶ It made products that were relevant to the local market.
❷ Unlike many of its competitors, it put social responsibility before image.
❸ It chose its price points carefully.

#39
Brands
Doing Good

'I think brands have actually got the potential to save the world. That's why I'm most interested in working there [with brands], because you vote with your credit card, and it's where you spend your money. It's [the area that's] going to get the investment and the growth. So, very simplistically, that for me is the sort of relationship I see with brands.'

Jeremy Brown

This, then, is the next step: brands doing good. It's not about an NGO or a charity or a brand appearing to do its bit for society and/or the environment. Instead, it's about doing business *and* doing good, about fusing the two together. Corporate social responsibility (CSR) used to be something that brands had to be seen to be doing. Now, it's one of the most efficient ways for a company to get its name out there and make authentic and meaningful brand connections. But I'm not talking about the obligatory, box-ticking CSR here. This is about a more basic philosophy, the cumulative effect of money well spent as a brand begins to grow.

I recently accepted a commission from Diageo, the multinational drinks company (Smirnoff and Guinness are but two of its big-name brands) based in London. It wanted me to help it gain some insights into the sub-Saharan market, where alcohol is not perceived in the same way as it is in the rest of the world. Spirits and beer are usually homemade, for example, while imported beer brands usually fail – with the exception of Guinness, that is. In addition, alcohol advertising was about to be banned in a number of African countries, so the alcohol giants were looking for new ways of creating much needed content. I did this by seeking out fresh, local talent and then using Diageo's money to help develop it. It took me a while to come to terms with the idea of selling alcohol in Africa – especially the ethical dimension – but I came to the conclusion that if I wasn't going to do it then somebody else would come along, take the company's money and perhaps not do any good with it. My mantra is accept the brand's money and help people with it. Perhaps this is the modern face of patronage.

When it comes to brands doing good, it's not just the front end of the business that has to be clean, but also the back end. It's a question of transparency. The tax-avoidance claims laid at the doors of such companies as Amazon, Google and Starbucks in 2013 had a huge impact on how these brands are perceived by the public. Likewise, think of the effect that the horsemeat scandal, also of 2013, had on such frozen-food brands as Findus. And no matter what the brand does to rectify the situation (back-pedal and begin to pay taxes, offer refunds for foodstuffs already purchased), it's usually too late: the damage has been done.

In an Unbrandable world, the one thing that is guaranteed to warm the heart of even the most cynical consumer is a brand doing some good. It's the simplest of ideas, but it works. Perhaps brands do have the power to change the world, to really make a difference.

'It's nice to buy a product and know that by buying it you're not only getting what you want but also doing some good. It might make me want to purchase special packages or promotional versions of the brand because I know it will go towards some good ... It's like a bonus towards how I perceive a brand and my purchase of that brand.'

DeAnna Forbes-Sanchez, teenage entrepreneur

#40
Unbrandable Places: The Mars Bar, New York

'In the 1980s New York was still a real city. By that I mean there were distinctive neighbourhoods and there were still "working" neighbourhoods. The transvestite prostitutes worked the streets late at night – their main clientele was men coming in just for this purpose, from New Jersey. On pleasant evenings after work these transvestites and transsexuals slept across from where I lived, out of doors on a metal ramp ... There were strange little bars and clubs but these were shabby and tucked in out-of-the-way places and you had to be kind of in the know to go to them. It was different then ... There are so many differences between then and now. I could go on and on – when graffiti began to be shown in galleries, for example. What it was like to hang out with Warhol ...'

Tama Janowitz, writer

Unfortunately, the Mars Bar is no more (although there have been rumours of it reopening, in the building that now stands in its place). This legendary East Village dive was closed for good in 2011 after the New York health department found 850 fruit flies in various parts of the bar and conditions conducive to infestation, including standing water on the floor and waterlogged wooden flooring. It was, to be honest, a bit of a shit hole, and that was before you even went near the bathrooms (which were, to say the least, properly rank). But no one went there for the cleanliness.

With a capacity of forty people, the Mars Bar was essentially an alcohol-fuelled community centre for local artists, musicians, 'Bowery Bums', drug dealers and the occasional punter with an animal of some description perched on his or her shoulder. The walls – behind the ever-present exhibition of local art – were covered in graffiti ('I can't believe I'm here again', 'Save a city, kill a yuppie'), and always reminded me of a Basquiat painting; the music on the juke box, meanwhile, was punk and more punk. Eventually, the building in which it stood was replaced with yet another expensive condo on top of a soulless bank.

The Mars Bar ran for twenty-seven years. It was an important spot, with a long cultural history, and represented far more than just a place where the locals got drunk. It was a window into what remained of New York's downtown scene.

#41
Unbrandable People: Roger Ballen

Roger is an American-born photographer based in Johannesburg. Best known for his images of the inhabitants of South African dorps (villages or small towns), and, more recently, for his work with the South African rap group Die Antwoord, Roger is Unbrandable not only because he refuses to work with brands, but also for his attitude towards his art.

'I come from an interesting background', Roger explains. 'I was part of the so-called hippy culture. My first degree was from the University of California, Berkeley; I graduated from there in the early 1970s. I'm a veteran of Woodstock, and grew up in New York City and so experienced the beat generation. I travelled to South Africa in the 1970s by travelling overland from Cairo to Cape Town, and after that I did a land trip from Istanbul to New Guinea. After that trip, I actually felt as though I understood human culture in some intrinsic way. I'm not saying I know every aspect, but after those trips I had some kind of handle on what humanity is about. Travelling by land with no money back then was a lot different, and I often think back to those trips. Travelling through Africa alone, I didn't see a phone that worked for nine months. My only means of expression was my photography. And so I focused on that to survive and to be creative.

'Talking about globalization and creativity today there are a couple of problems that come to mind. First, concrete experience has a far greater impact on the human psyche than a virtual experience. And you see that in art. A lot of art seems to be like advertising: it doesn't seem to

have any human-condition substance to it. To me, it's about what
is the final purpose of art? It is to convey a meaning, and this meaning
should have some deeper significance. The other problem we face
with globalization is that the ideas that we created in the 1970s about
corporatism and consumption – those were new and revolutionary in
their own way. What's happened over the last decade is that the global
corporate sector has camouflaged itself in all sorts of ways. So you're cool
and neat and smart and creative – on a Mac. Go to the supermarket and
all the products are "natural", but what does that mean? The terminology
has become very confusing, the way we express ourselves and think of
freedom, creativity, individualism and spirituality.'

#42
Unbranded Brands: Mojang/*Minecraft*

Until it was bought by Microsoft at the end of 2014 (more on that below), Mojang was an independent video-game developer based in Stockholm. It is best known as the company behind the game *Minecraft*, with which it has single-handedly reinvented how video games are developed. By initially releasing the game in a developmental, 'alpha' version, Mojang succeeded in harnessing the power of gamers themselves, using them as testers and allowing them to have a say in how the game was designed. The full version of *Minecraft* – an 'open world' game in which players are more or less free to choose how they play – was released in 2011, and since then it has sold more than 54 million copies. Its followers, some of whom have made videos and online comics about their *Minecraft* experiences, couldn't care less about brands. In fact, it's a classic Unbrandable brand – and one that has changed the entire gaming industry.

'For me, "indie" … is a kinda concept about people making games for the sake of making games – exploring games as an art form, perhaps. I think a lot of the large studios make games to make money, or make games to make a sequel or to make a brand. To make a game just for the sake of making a game – that is the definition of "indie" for me.'

Markus 'Notch' Persson, creator of Minecraft *and founder of Mojang*

128

It was as this book was being edited that Mojang decided to sell out to Microsoft – and I mean that in the strongest sense of the phrase. I was asked by my editor whether I wanted to include the entry at all, but the truth is that it's a perfect example of something Unbrandable becoming subsumed by the mainstream. The question I kept returning to was what was Microsoft actually buying? Was it interested only in *Minecraft*, or was it trying to buy into the whole ethos and mindset of Mojang? Which, of course, is something that you can't really do – one of the main philosophies of this book. Money doesn't mean everything in an Unbrandable world.

'*Minecraft*'s lack of guidance and the freedom of choice it offers distinguishes it from the patronizing nature of most mainstream games. It is also a tool for creativity, which can't be said of most other games.'

Casius Stone, former gamer

What lay behind Mojang's success?

1. *Minecraft* was a game changer, literally, because it was based on a simple premise: do what you want.
2. The company took a huge risk launching the game while it was still in development.
3. It listened to its fans and, as a result, created a unique connection between fan and game.

#43
New Methods of Research

'The client often wants ten interviews by the end of the day, and I'm like, I can't do that – I can't guarantee it. If I'm going to start a conversation with someone, I'm going to keep on chatting … My turnarounds are pretty quick, but often it'll take me two days to speak to ten people, or maybe even three if it ends up being proper conversations. I try to be as authentic as I can, with the car that I drive and the look that I have. I try to make sure that I don't wear a brand that could be associated with whatever it is I'm researching, so they can't position me – I find that people a lot more honest with me [when I do that].'

Leroy Tulip

The digital revolution has changed not only the way brands are marketed and sold but also the way research is conducted. On the one hand, the old models of marketing and research are now redundant. They don't work. On the other, both are imperative if you want to make a connection with your audience – Unbrandable or otherwise. Insightful research that informs authentic content is the way forward. No more focus groups (hallelujah!). What is the point of testing an idea after it's been realized? In any case, what often happens is that the data are manipulated to fit the brief and please the client. The truth is that the majority of good brand communication has a lot of up-front research behind it: without the insights that can be gained from such research, it can be hard to understand exactly what makes people tick. Done properly, research can be an incredibly valuable exercise, and more emphasis should be placed on trying to understand why people behave the way they do. The act of branding has been compressed into a validation process, and that's not really what we should be spending our money on. We should be spending it on gaining insights into consumer behaviour from real-world data. It's obvious, really.

'Often, "new" methods of research are met with a sigh by seasoned practitioners. Research is a science; it's tried and tested, and when used properly it works. Technology, consumerism and other influences may have changed the way an audience wants to engage with a brand, but ultimately the only way to stay relevant is by observing and listening. Social media and online analytics provide an almost unfathomable pool of data, but so did [environmental psychologist Paco] Underhill's thousands of hours of video.

For me, useful insight comes from unstructured research. We want people to behave naturally and we want them to break things; we just need to make sure we're there when it happens. And that chaotic approach requires more planning than structured research. For example, if you want to know how kids consume media and brands, don't ask them about industry categories. Ask them to throw all their sneakers, clothes, books, CDs, movies, technology on the living-room floor and sort them into piles that mean something to them. Chances are that "stuff my best mate bought for me" and "things that cheer me up" are going to be a whole lot more useful than knowing what they think of paranormal romance.

If you want a kid to tell you what they think of your game, don't spend a fortune and then see if it sells. Create a paper version of it and test it in week one. Scary, hey? Because before you even started coding you might find out your idea needs a whole lot of thinking. But it's worth it; these moments help us reach out through genuine innovation that fits a need or creates a desire.'

Peter Robinson, researcher and heritage-brand specialist

Research today should take into account three things. First (and most importantly) there's the audience. Gone are the days of the career panellist; this new-and-improved research era is all about the 'involved consumer'. You want some feedback on your product? Give it to the consumer! Just look at what Google did with its Google Glass wearable technology, or Mojang with its video game *Minecraft* (see previous entry): find the consumers who have an opinion, give or sell them an early version of your product, and create a feedback loop. Secondly, there's the speed of modern life: email, mobile phones, social media, online communities and clients who need answers the day before yesterday. All of this has meant that research has had to adapt to keep up; now, it's very much about the fast and accurate interpretation and application of data. Thirdly, there's globalization. Research must result in products that are capable of jumping borders: in a connected world, the tastes of a fifteen-year-old in London are just as likely to match those of a seventeen-year-old in Rio de Janeiro as they are those of the London teenager's friend next door.

'When it comes to evaluating anything new, asking people in market research works about as well as all other future forecasting pseudoscience, which is to say not very well at all. Organizations that solicit consumers' opinions of their intended activity and

allow the resulting consensus view to inform their actions are spending money in deluded hope, rather than because such market research works. Customers don't know how they will react in a real-world context to a proposition. What's more, there is abundant evidence in psychology to prove that the process of asking people what they think creates a different context that exerts its own influences on what people say they think.'

Philip Graves, writer

#44
Words with the Shaman: Leroy Tulip

I was introduced to Leroy at a book launch in Johannesburg, and I think it's fair to say that he's one of the most interesting blokes I've met in a long time: part researcher, part anthropologist, part hot-rod and motorbike enthusiast. Which is, I reckon, a pretty Unbrandable combination.

One of Leroy's earliest engagements with the world of research came while he was studying sports administration and marketing as an undergraduate in Johannesburg. Having chosen a research module as part of his studies, he realized that his part-time job as a waiter in a bar in Melville – at the time a trendy Johannesburg suburb – gave him access to the very stuff of research: people. 'All the time I was engaging and learning how to ask the right questions in order to find out what the customer wanted', he explains. 'I prided myself on being the kind of waiter that would take you on a journey, so if you didn't know what to drink I'd suggest something. The whole "upsell" process. I realized that perhaps I should take a few notes, you know, so I started to take the customer's picture, write down their insights, why they drank Windhoek lager or smoked Luckies …' This was around the time that Lucky Strike sponsored a series of concerts by the West Coast hip-hop act Cypress Hill, which resulted in the brand getting a lot of traction. And so Leroy started passing on the information he was gathering to the likes of South African Breweries and British American Tobacco.

It was also through his job at the bar that Leroy was introduced to the guys from Instant Grass. Founded by Ian Calvert and Greg Potterton, Instant Grass is an innovative South African insights agency with offices in Johannesburg and Cape Town. It was the first such agency to arm its on-the-ground researchers – in Instant Grass's case, a group of young, highly networked trendspotters known as 'grasses' – with camera phones, in order to get real-time insights into the mass market. Leroy served Greg at the bar one day, and decided to find out more about him. As for Greg, says Leroy, '[He] was like, "Let's have a chat. We're thinking of starting this agency …"' Eventually, Leroy became Instant Grass's first Johannesburg grass. 'I was twenty-five or twenty-six at the time', he explains, 'and still living like a student, so I had access to that world. I worked full time with the agency for a good three or four years.'

Leroy's father was a local politician. He used to do a lot of work in the townships, at a time when whites weren't supposed to enter such places, and Leroy would accompany him on his visits. His father would drive them to their destination in his classic Volvo coupé. 'My dad would use that car because it's quite distinguishable and people would accept him in that, like he wouldn't be showing off or anything. My dad would do crazy things with me … When the Queen came out here and they had tea at the Gallagher Estate [near Johannesburg], I went to tea with my dad. And then straight after that he took me to a shabeen in a township, and he's like, "That's that, but this is this." That's the kind of life I had.' Leroy still drives the Volvo, and often uses it when he's working in the townships. He drives up, and the car starts a conversation.

When Leroy started working at Instant Grass, he began to realize that market research was a far more structured activity than he'd assumed. Keen to learn more, he enrolled on a post-graduate course at the Vega School of Brand Leadership in Johannesburg. 'After that, Ian Calvert found me a job at Ogilvy [& Mather, also in Johannesburg], in a department called Field Brand Investigation. Then I had the idea of speaking to creators and conducting research relevant to creativity … mainly to keep the creatives inspired but also to make sure that their communication was relevant. The idea was to do lots of short tests all the time to make sure that we were always on strategy, to get the job done quicker.' Leroy then spent the next year and a half working for 'brown bottled beer', Fanta and Sprite – work that took him to almost every township in South Africa. He remembers this time as an incredible learning experience: 'It was just unbelievable.'

The conversation turns to the subject of how the market has changed since the digital revolution, and more specifically to how South Africa has changed. Leroy begins by talking about the South Africa of ten to fifteen years ago. 'We kind of felt like the underdog,' he explains, 'that anything foreign was better than ours … So if something was imported, it was definitely seen as something better. We weren't really proud of our music, or proud of our fashion, or proud of anything that we really delivered.' But, thinks Leroy, things are changing. 'I would say [that today's] sixteen- to twenty-four-year-olds … are very proudly South African.' Coupled with this newfound sense of pride is a spirit of innovation, especially within the black community, with local designers, creatives and marketers starting their own companies – the only other option being to work as an intern in the hope of getting a poorly paid job at the end of it all. The message from these young entrepreneurs is clear: forget about the big guy – let's get out there and do it on our own.

There's also a sense that young South Africans are keen to make whatever they do relevant to their own cultural DNA – a truly Unbrandable aspiration. A sense of belonging is equally as noticeable, with even those young people who have moved out of the townships returning to the family home at weekends to renew their sense of community. They often bring presents with them (and are always sending money back home), and, once there, will make a point of buying from the little guy on the corner selling peanuts or whatnot. By way of an example, Leroy tells me about 'Mogodu Mondays', mogodu being a traditional African dish made of tripe. 'There's a township down the road in Alex,' he begins, 'and there's a gathering on a Monday night where the locals who have moved out come back in and hang out at this bar. The locals were like, "Oh, let's do some traditional dishes", because they aren't really eaten as much as they used to be. So it's their little tap back to tradition. It's just an amazing thing: even as this mass market is emerging and, for want of a better word, becoming Westernized, it wants to hold on to and celebrate its heritage – by having Mogodu Mondays.'

We return to the subject of advertising and branding. These days, the public spend a lot of time and money on maintaining their chosen 'brand personalities'. In turn, the brands are devoting more and more time to developing platforms from which to speak to their customers,

adapting their behaviour to fit different markets. 'People are starting
to become aware of [this tactic]', observes Leroy, 'and if it's appropriate
or not in these spaces. Take Apple, for example. From the conversations
I've had with people, a lot of them are finding Apple to be a bully brand,
and they don't like bullies. And unfortunately they are kind of locked in.'
This leaves a gap for a competitor to fill: when a brand behaves badly,
the customer will just turn to a brand that is going to treat them properly.
Ultimately, consumers want to be treated in the same way as they treat
their favourite brands – with respect. There also has to be trust on
both sides.

'If a consumer doesn't love you the way you want them to love you,'
Leroy continues, 'it doesn't mean that they're not loving you. A good
example of this is when brands go, "Oh, we've only got so many likes on
our Facebook page." Those "likes" could mean something completely
different, but [the consumers] are engaging with your brand on another
level, on another platform … So, instead of having five major platforms
that you're working off, have five and then five sub-platforms within that,
so you've got twenty-five platforms. Just nurture all these little points of
interaction [with the consumer] and be each of these things.'

Which is all excellent Unbrandable advice.

Haas & Hahn (Jeroen Koolhaas and Dre Urhahn) are two Dutch artists from Amsterdam (that place again!) who have been creating large-scale murals and other public artworks since 2005. Although they are best known for Favela Painting, a series of works created in the favelas of Rio de Janeiro, they have carried out similar projects in other parts of the world. While I was on the road for this book I stopped off in Philadelphia to check out Philly Painting, a project that saw the duo join forces with a group of local youth to paint several blocks of a North Philadelphia neighbourhood. I have included Haas & Hahn in this book because although Favela Painting was created for social rather than commercial reasons (as is most of their work), it has nevertheless been featured in the ads for several global brands.

While Favela Painting was driven by Haas & Hahn themselves, the project in Philadelphia was initiated by the Philadelphia Mural Arts Program, one of the largest public arts organizations in the United States. In 2010, during an exhibition at the Storefront for Art and Architecture in New York about their work in Rio, Haas & Hahn were invited to Philadelphia to see if a project like Favela Painting could work in a large, post-industrial American city. 'We had no idea how to pull it off,' Hahn tells me as we take our seats in an Amsterdam bar one day, 'but were intrigued by the question, so we said, "Yes, we can!" and moved our operations to a North Philly neighbourhood. It took us a while to get a good feel of how we should approach this completely different visual and social situation. As soon as the crew started painting, everything fell into place and now we are very proud with the result, especially the fact that the project continues in our absence.'

At the start of the project the locals were a bit wary of these two funny Dutch guys wandering around the 'hood, and a lot of people assumed they were cops. But as soon as the project took off and people saw what it was about, as well as how dedicated Haas & Hahn were to their work, they started getting lots of questions, comments and even praise. 'The key to the [project's] success', observes Hahn, 'was the fact that we had hired a 100 per cent local crew. There was an incredible need for jobs in the neighbourhood, and we were sorry we couldn't hire more people. The fact that people saw their own friends, family or neighbours handling large lifts and working hard to make the neighbourhood look better had an amazing impact on the community … People stopped on the street and started talking about the history of the area. Commuters parked their cars and started to walk around in awe.'

One of the questions posed by this book is whether it's possible for Western culture to move forwards without the involvement of brands. '[That's] such an interesting question,' says Hahn, 'because our culture is so brand-focused and all actions are so brand-driven. We've noticed that even when unbranded, our projects tend to become brands themselves … A Dutch shoe manufacturer, for example, made a Philly Painting sneaker. Instead of putting their brand names on our projects, the reverse happened and our project name ended up on their products. Not to mention all the companies that use images of our Brazilian project in their ads. It's flattering, but they might think about actually supporting the very same work … The bottom line is that brands have a lot of power and sometimes seem like the only way to realize a large creative idea.'

If it weren't for the very visible need to shift product, a tendency to avoid controversy and the strict guidelines, brands and branding would provide a great platform for creativity. Far too few brand managers understand that street cred comes from giving creative freedom to your sponsored party and then taking a more humble and intelligent role when they achieve success, while resisting the urge to scatter logos everywhere. 'That's why crowdfunding is pretty exciting,' adds Hahn, 'generating project budget without any other agenda than the creator's creativity.'

#46
Unbranded Brands: NPR and PBS

NPR (National Public Radio) and PBS (Public Broadcasting Service) are not-for-profit media organizations based in the United States. Both were founded in 1970. NPR syndicates news and cultural programming – some of which it produces itself – to a network of some 900 public radio stations across the country. PBS is NPR's television equivalent, providing programmes to more than 350 public television stations nationwide. Unlike NPR, however, PBS has no central production arm or news department of its own; instead, all of its content is either created by or produced under contract with other parties.

With reputations for unbiased and authentic programming, both organizations have definitely got what it takes to make a genuine connection with the Unbrandables. In an era of media fragmentation, press release-based journalism and sound bites, NPR in particular is known for its in-depth, quality news programmes – something of a rarity in the United States, where many of the commercial networks have strong political affiliations (think Fox and its support of the Republican Party). Likewise, PBS is widely regarded as America's most-trusted national institution. It's not all revolutionary rhetoric, though: PBS broadcasts such popular programmes as *Sherlock* and *Downton Abbey* as part of its *Masterpiece* series, which is partly funded by Viking River Cruises and Ralph Lauren. There's always a brand or two lurking somewhere in the background …

Why they work:

1. They are independent sources of news.
2. They appeal to a wide range of tastes, providing both left-field and more popular programmes.
3. Non-commercial culture is a vital part of a balanced society.

#47
Unbrandable People: Beppe Grillo

An Italian comedian, blogger and political activist, Beppe Grillo is something of a phenomenon. Never afraid to name corrupt brands and politicians as part of his comedy set, he became a political activist almost by accident. In the late 1980s Grillo was effectively banned from appearing on Italian state television after making fun of Italy's then prime minister, Bettino Craxi – who was eventually convicted of corruption. Undeterred, he took his show on the road and began touring relentlessly, targeting whichever establishment figures had caught his attention (by doing something wrong or corrupt). Seeing the opportunities presented by the Internet and social media, he started expressing his political views by means of a blog, and his popularity exploded.

In 2007 Grillo organized the first V-Day Celebration (the 'V' stands for *vaffanculo*, or 'fuck off'), the first political rally in Italy promoted entirely by means of social media and the blogosphere. Attended by some 2 million people, the rally saw Grillo name and shame more than twenty politicians who had been convicted of such crimes as corruption, tax evasion and even abetting a murder. Dirty deeds indeed! In 2009 he started his own political party, Movimento 5 Stelle (Five Star Movement), which, at the Italian general election of 2013, won 25.5 per cent of the vote for the Chamber of Deputies. This despite the fact that Grillo himself was slated by the newspapers and other Berlusconi-owned media outlets.

Grillo represents a genuine alternative to the corrupt political mainstream. He gave the disassociated a voice, and power to those

who felt betrayed by the system; he also succeeded in breaking through the tribal barriers that define Italian politics, getting votes from both left and right. The world is growing tired of corrupt politicians and their fat-cat business cronies, and Grillo spearheaded a global wave of dissent.
He is a truly Unbrandable guy.

'I think that Grillo is a fantastic man. He's been denouncing for many years the corruption in our political system, as well as criticizing what dishonest but powerful people have done wrong to our beautiful country. He has, of course, a great sense of humour, but he's not a clown. I personally did not vote for him because I thought our country needed a steady government, but I would certainly vote Grillo in the next election – and many people would do the same, I think.'

Franca Silvi Taylor, my Italian nonna

#48
Unbrandable Places: Forte Prenestino, Rome

I am lucky enough to have an Italian grandmother (you've just met her, in fact; see previous entry), and one Sunday afternoon while I was visiting family in Italy my twin aunts, Lynda and Ellen, took me to visit Forte Prenestino. A late nineteenth-century military fort, one of fifteen that surround the city of Rome, it was never used to its full potential and was abandoned almost from the start. On 1 May 1986 a group of local youths decided to occupy the fort, and then spent several years restructuring and adapting the building for social use. It is now a hive of activity, consisting of arts workshops, a cinema, a restaurant and café, a recording studio, a screen-printing room, a joinery, a gym, a record label, a tattoo studio and a bar; on the day of my visit, the last of these was crammed with people watching Roma vs Lazio. Although technically illegal, Forte Prenestino is a real community, with a proper heart and soul. This is what makes it so Unbrandable, especially in such a beautiful yet extremely tourist-orientated city as Rome. The world needs more places like this.

#49
An Unbrandable Moment: *Trainspotting*

'Brands: I like – familiarity; hate – ubiquity.'

Irvine Welsh

When the Scottish novelist, playwright and short-story writer Irvine Welsh delivered the manuscript of his debut novel to his publishers in 1992, they told him that it probably wouldn't sell many copies. At best, they said, it might become one of those edgy, underground cult classics that a handful of people read and then mutter about among themselves. Little did they know … The subsequent success of *Trainspotting*, which revolves around the heroin-fuelled misadventures of some of the inhabitants of the Edinburgh district of Leith, is an almost textbook example of the power of the Unbrandables – of how something from the subcultural depths can enter the mainstream without anyone seeing it coming.

Fast forward some twenty years and I'm standing outside the Valvona & Crolla café in Edinburgh, waiting for the man himself to arrive. It's a gloriously sunny day, and Irvine wants to take me on a tour of his beloved Leith, so he can show me some of the sights that made it into *Trainspotting*, as well as where he spent part of his childhood. Knowing the book as I do, and having been to Leith in the 1980s, it soon becomes apparent as we start our tour that Leith has changed immensely; it's now full of bars and restaurants and boutique hotels in converted warehouses.

The dock area used to be full of whores, pimps, junkies and drug dealers. 'Now there's a fucking Malmaison!' Irvine observes. 'It was the kind of place where anybody who came into town and wanted to get up to something naughty was sent. Sometimes it didne work out for them and sometimes it did. It was always the sleazy part of town. And now it's just that thing about yuppies and water: wherever they see water they want to congregate around it.'

But you'd have to say that it's changed for the better. It's easy to romanticize the sleaze – something that Irvine has often been accused of doing – but before the gentrification kicked in a lot of the buildings were properly fucked. Now there are signs of money and life. The flipside to all this regeneration is that a lot of the social problems that were here have simply been moved to other parts of the city, often to where the inhabitants already have it tough. This is the kind of double-edged sword that comes free with every inner-city regeneration dream. It's a bit like the Banksy stencil of the Hispanic maid sweeping the dirt under the wall.

A yummy-mummy type runs out of her front garden, stops us in the street with an 'Oh my God!' and goes on to tell us that she was just reading one of Irvine's books in her kitchen and now here she is, standing in front of him! He smiles, says 'Great stuff!' and she returns to her house, beaming. He really is a man of Leith. His writing is a product of the place, too, but it's also evolved out of street culture. 'Street culture hasn't *influenced* my work,' notes Irvine, 'more like it's the totality of it. Just with the changes we've had in the last twenty years it's harder to find unmodified street culture that isn't media culture, that hasn't been subsumed into the media. And that's why I'm somewhat stuck in an eighties time warp when I do my writing.'

Back then it was possible for street culture to exist without instantly being absorbed by the media, to be used for some commercial reason before being spat back out. To some extent there is still some original street culture in Edinburgh – in such estates as Burdiehouse, for example – but Irvine is way too old to be a part of that now. 'I just know that those little fuckers are having a great time and doing some wonderful things', he observes. Besides, as soon as you're old enough to publish books or shoot films, you immediately become part of the whole media-culture-circus-factory thing, whether you like it or not. We both agree what a shame it is that street culture no longer has a chance to stay underground before it's relentlessly commoditized and then sold back to the kids. 'Street culture *is* culture. Everything I learned, about football, music, clothes, drugs, girls, I learned through my peers. I certainly didn't get it from school.'

When the street that Irvine was growing up on was earmarked for demolition as part of a slum clearance, the council moved the Welshes into a prefab in Pilton, a residential area of north Edinburgh, which was fantastic in the summer because of all the space and the huge garden, but almost impossible to keep warm in the winter. The prefabs were also extremely damp, and the young Irvine developed bronchitic symptoms, as did many of his friends. When the Pilton prefabs were demolished, the Welshes were moved to a maisonette on the nearby Muirhouse estate. 'Muirhouse had a bad reputation from the mid-eighties onwards,' remembers Irvine, 'as it became ghettoized after the Right to Buy legislation creamed off the best council houses and mass unemployment hit the place, but growing up there in the seventies was brilliant. You knew everybody in your street, and played football all day and all night long. The community was so tight … You don't need CCTV and databases and loads of cops to make things safe, you just need a sense of community.'

It turns out that Irvine was a bit of a scribbler as a child, and would draw, paint and write over everything. At primary school he was teased by the other kids and harassed by his teacher for covering his maths books in drawings of monsters and symbols. He hated maths but loved the design of numbers, and would often make up new ones; soon, he was developing narratives for his creations and writing stories about them. 'I was always moved to express myself creatively. Unfortunately, it gets knocked out of you. Schools back then – and it's probably the same now – are set up to meet the needs of society and the economy and function as bureaucracies. They don't want some snotty little day-dreaming cunt creating his alternative universe. They want a neat, tidy, obedient little chap who will do as he's told, work hard at his sums and not cause them any bother. And go on to work diligently in one of the local or global enterprises.'

Things improved for Irvine at secondary school, mainly because the teachers had bigger fish to fry in trying to contain the wannabe gangster fuckers, and were less concerned about slightly problematic would-be artists. This was when he realized that if he didn't draw attention to himself he could go to the lessons he enjoyed – English, art and geography – and sleep or bunk off for the rest. 'I had one teacher, Mrs Tait in English, who was very good. She encouraged me to write, and pushed decent books my way, not necessarily the ones on the official curriculum. If you go to a large comprehensive on a sink estate, and you have artistic tendencies/aspirations, you need teachers like that or you'll go down.'

When I was a teenager it was people like Irvine, Tama Janowitz and Martin Amis who inspired me to write. Their books actually spoke to me, and the fact that they even existed was an indication that I had to begin writing my own stories, about my own world. These writers were also documenting a side to the 1980s that was firmly rooted in Western *sub*culture, and that was something that fascinated me in a way I knew I couldn't ignore. Irvine's influences included the people he grew up around, the people on his estate. 'If you live next door to a merchant seaman, or a waitress, or a postman, or a thief, or a whisky bonds worker, you're going to get interesting stories. I was influenced more by the energy of musicians like Iggy Pop initially, then more narrative ones like Lou Reed, Nick Cave and Shane MacGowan, who complemented the books I was reading: Russian lit like Dostoyevsky and Tolstoy; English like Orwell, Waugh, Austen; Scottish like Grassic Gibbon, [James] Kelman, [Alasdair] Gray; and, most of all, American, such as [Charles] Bukowski, [William] Burroughs, [William T.] Volman, [Philip K.] Dick, etc.' He also became aware of the way in which the environment people lived in, the type of house they occupied and the sort of work they did were central to how they told their stories.

The conversation returns to the subject of *Trainspotting*, and in particular to the fact that so many people tuned into the book and got wrapped up in the alternative zeitgeist it offered. To say that the book's success took the publishers by surprise is something of an understatement. 'They kept reprinting the fucker a thousand at a time', explains Irvine. 'I was like, just print 20,000 or 100,000 – stop fannying around!' What's really interesting about the book's success is that when it sold its first 1,000 copies, Irvine was seen as this local hero; when it sold 10,000, people were still chuffed that the book was doing so well, that it was mutating into something bigger; but when it sold 100,000 copies, people began to feel that something had been taken away from them, that their culture had been hijacked by people who knew nothing about the world portrayed in the book's pages. 'When it sold a million it was like, "He's fucking sold out!", but it's basically the same book; you can't change it once it's out there. You're stuck with it and you can't take it back. It's a weird, weird thing. The more it sold, the more it became this mask and the more it was removed from the culture it was originally about.'

We talk about how it would be very difficult (impossible?) to get *Trainspotting* published today because there isn't a place on the shelf for it: everything is just so marketed now. Go into any bookshop and you'll find a place for crime, a place for romance, a place for so-called literary fiction. But, says Irvine, 'There's not really a place for Scottish schemies on smack – there's no section there. Underground fiction these days is about being commissioned by the *New Yorker* to write about checking into an expensive treatment clinic. The whole thing has changed. Publishing needs another punk rock-ish, acid house-type thing to get it back to something good. Most of the fiction I find interesting now is on the Net. It comes from sites I find interesting, and I'd rather [look online] than browse in a bookshop. It goes back to that two-tier system. The good stuff is happening online, and … some of that stuff will make it into print – that next tier, if you like. But because of the time-lapse in publishing, by the time that kind of stuff becomes an artefact you can hold, there will be more contemporary stuff happening online.'

We end our tour in a Leith pub. A motley crew of locals is watching the horse racing on a couple of large screens fixed high up on the walls. Irvine tells me what he wants to drink and nips off to the bogs. I walk up to the bar and order two pints of lime and soda. The barman scoffs at me. Not only am I English but also I'm ordering a couple of 'poof' drinks. He is being a proper arse, but his face quickly changes from right moody to smiley fucker when he spies Irvine coming out of the toilets and walking over to where I'm waiting for the drinks. I tell him to grab a seat and that I'll be with him in a sec. The barman nods at our Irv and then forces a smile for me. This, then, is the image I'll leave you with: me and Irvine Welsh drinking very soft drinks in a very not-soft pub in Leith. Chemicals, anyone? Not on yer nelly.

Released in 2007, Annie Leonard's film *The Story of Stuff* is a game-changing, mind-blowing, thought-provoking documentary about the realities of consumption that everyone should see. It was a major influence on parts of this book (especially #12, 'Manufactured Desire', page 52) and opened my eyes to many things. I managed to track Annie down to Berkeley, California, where I asked her for her thoughts on all things brand-related.

Annie, a proponent of sustainability and executive director of Greenpeace USA, has a teenage daughter, and so has seen for herself the way in which young people are indoctrinated into the consumer culture. 'I see it all the time', she explains. But, she thinks, things are changing. 'I see a decreasing desire for the brands … As our social fabric and social identity and attachment with a community – all these other ways that we use to find meaning and identity – as those deteriorated over the preceding decades, people were so hungry to find and demonstrate their meaning and identity through brands. [But] I think we realized that, after working our butts off to pay for that stuff, it doesn't work … so I see people turning away from that commoditized sense of identity as they hunger for real senses of identity.'

We begin to discuss the fact that many people are looking for more sincere, authentic and effective ways to find community and meaning, rather than just buying some expensive brand to display in public. 'I'm very hopeful about this turn away from stuff', observes Annie. 'It's not everywhere, as I was recently in a duty-free shop in Dubai, and it was enough to make you want to blow your head off, to see these people just going nuts for consumption. But in a lot of places it's true: the promises that the consumption peddlers offered didn't pay out.'

I decide to play devil's advocate by suggesting that many people believe that wanting things is part of what makes us human. 'It's not just innate … We're all so bombarded by these messages associating these products with certain lifestyles … telling us to shop shop shop. It drives me nuts when people say, "Well, it's human nature to want this new stuff." It's because of these messages! What if we were bombarded with thousands of messages a day telling us to be kind to one another and to the planet? We'd have a totally different cultural undercurrent.' But how do we get the Unbrandable message out there? How can the Unbrandables make a difference, help speed up this much-needed change? 'When people ask me if that kind of change is possible, I say it's not just possible, it's inevitable. We have a different situation now to the hippies in the 1960s, who were forsaking consumerism for spiritual reasons; we have a biological and actual physical imperative. It is simply impossible to continue to consume at the rate we are consuming. At the moment we are using one and a half planet's worth of resources each year and producing one and a half times the waste that the planet can assimilate.'

The question, then, is not *if* change is going to occur, but how? 'I think this change is either going to happen by design or by disaster,' observes Annie, 'but either way, change is happening. If it's change by design we're going to have to rethink, rebuild a lot of aspects of our economy and society … Some parts of our lives will be harder and other parts will be better, but it is definitely going to be different for our grandchildren than it was for us. But if we don't get strategic and proactive about it, consumer society is still going to change – but it's going to happen by disaster, which will be a lot uglier, a lot less just.'

One of the issues that is often overlooked in discussions about consumption is inequality. We live in a world in which, on the one hand, millions of people are chronically hungry and dangerously under-consuming, and yet, on the other, millions more are chronically obese and over-consuming. So, if we want to maintain our current levels of consumption, part of the cost is denying other people the things they need simply to survive. 'When they realize that is the choice,' adds Annie, 'most people do not want this consumption apartheid. Most people don't want that grossly unequal society. If we want the world to be more fair than it is now – which is what I hope everyone wants – and since we recognize the ecological limitations we face, the only conclusion is that we've just got to scale back our consumption. I was reading the Millennium Ecosystem Assessment [a United Nations-initiated report on the consequences for human well-being of changes to the ecosystem] … and learned that all the fish populations that are commercially fished right now will collapse by 2040, if current trajectories continue. That is a bummer for those of us who like sushi, but far worse for the millions of people who survive on subsistence fishing.'

Here, Annie makes a very interesting point about what all this change might involve. 'In terms of consumption,' she explains, 'we're lucky because the change that we want – which is for people to focus less on material being and more on health and social fabric and community and recreation and music and nature and all these things – that change is not only required by ecological limits but it's more fun. We're so lucky! We're not saying make this change and it's going to suck. We're saying make this change and its going to be better! The change we have to make will lead to greater, longer-lasting happiness. How fortuitous is it that the very thing we need to do to survive on this planet is also that which can bring us lasting happiness?'

But what about the argument bounced back by the producers and the brands – that all this consumption and mass-production is driven by the consumer? If there were no market, say the producers, there'd be no products. We are peddled the lie that the market, the consumer, dictates what is produced, but the real power lies with those who decide what gets made and how. 'If I want a cell phone, a radio or a computer,' says Annie, 'which are perfectly valid things to want, I want one not linked to worker-health issues, and not linked to conflict minerals. But that's not on the menu; I can't pick that because it's not there! I think it's driven by the corporate executives wanting the greatest profits.'

It's not just Annie who thinks this way. The American academic Thomas Princen has written a series of articles challenging the 'myth of the sovereign consumer', the idea that the system is driven by consumer desire. The reality, of course, is very different: brands produce whatever is going to make them the most money, and use relentless advertising to convince us it's what we want. 'In California', notes Annie, 'there is a law that the chemical industry got on the books, that says all children's pyjamas have to be treated with a flame retardant – which happens to contain neurotoxins. I don't know of any mother who wants her child's pyjamas soaked in neurotoxins. It is not consumer demand; that is totally bogus. In fact, I would challenge you to find any time that consumer demand alone changed anything. No major change has come about just because people shopped differently; it was because a bunch of activists did the digging to find out about hazardous components, and organized a strategic campaign that may have included advocating for different shopping habits, but also included media campaigns, lobbying for policies and other tactics. This shows that the consumer is *not* king. [The person] who *is* king, but not using that power, is the citizen. If we step out of our consumer self and into our citizen self and change the rules and laws and policies – that's how we're going to get these companies to change.'

Nuff said.

#51
No One Really Knows Anything

'I was just clearing things, you know, like you clear things; I was saving things, you know, like you save things; I was looking at things, [and] I found all these casting tapes for [my film] *American History X* **[1998] – Adrien Brody, Jack Black, Chloë Sevigny, Terrence Howard, Jamie Foxx, Vince Vaughn ... I could not believe the names! Some I remembered, some I did not ... I'm not well; it's crazy ... I thought I was good at casting! Nobody knows anything!'**

Tony Kaye

I have often been in a meeting and wondered, does anyone really know what's going on? In fact, it's moments like these when I can't help thinking that most people are just blagging their way through life – especially in the advertising and branding industries. But 'nobody knows anything' is one of the most powerful, progressive and Unbrandable places to start from, because (a) it's true, and (b) it means that anything is possible. I'm not saying that there aren't people out there who know what they're doing – there are, and some of them are in this book – but many of today's brands and agencies are just busking it, just making it up as they go along. They don't have a proper strategy; they don't really understand the space they need to exist in; and, thanks to the fact that some of them have a lot of money to throw around, they just charge ahead and steamroller their way through to the customer. But it's only the brands with a genuine story that enjoy any kind of longevity, and this is down to their customers. They exist because their customers allow them to, and you don't get to that state of affairs by making it up as you go along.

'We were told when we began writing [Danish political drama] *Borgen* **that the show would definitely not travel. This would be something that perhaps Sweden and Norway would buy out of politeness, because of brotherly, neighbourly feelings towards Denmark. And now we've sold the show to eighty countries.'**

Adam Price, screenwriter and producer

It's both the blessing and the curse of our generation: the need to be successful at everything we do. People used to be content with having hobbies and pastimes, one of which might have involved doing something arty, and there is absolutely nothing wrong with that. Most successful creatives have got to where they are today because of a love of doing something for the sake of it. And because what they do is authentic, people like it, are able to connect with it, and the word spreads organically. Most new content, however, is immediately labelled as 'great'. Take any mainstream television programme aimed at the youth market. Not only is it quick to jump on any 'cool' bandwagon rolling past, but also each and every one of its presenters is conditioned to proclaim every 5 minutes or so that something or someone is 'so cool', 'amazing', 'really wicked', 'brilliant' – usually in reference to some lame-o urban pop act or mindless Hollywood fare. This is the extent of the cultural vision: everything in youth-media land is brilliant. But if everything is brilliant, then everything is also total shite. Without the bad you can't see the good, and without constructive criticism there's no real progression. Which brings us back to our starting point: that no one really knows anything – especially, it would seem, in the film industry, which is increasingly reliant on the world of comics for its successes …

'The American comics industry – which is all that is left these days, effectively – it doesn't seem to have had a new idea in decades. All of the genuine creators that it once had, it alienated them or drove them to embittered retirement and finally death. You have to remember that, with the comics industry, you are talking about something that was set up in the 1920s by American entrepreneurs such as Legs Diamond, Mayer Lansky – the "original gangsters", as I believe the youngsters like to phrase it these days. It was set up purely as a cover for bootlegging. The ethics of the comics industry have not changed since those days when they were cheating Jerry Siegel and Joe Shuster, who were two teenagers from Cleveland who had created Superman.'

Alan Moore, writer

#52
Unbrandable People: Jennifer M.

Jennifer M. refuses to buy anything that's been in the media or the public eye; she won't ever be told what to do. She reads, listens, consumes at her own pace. Books, films, music – whatever. She lives in the East Village of New York in a rented one-bedroom walk-up and works in a call centre (or 'hell hole', as she calls it) and as a part-time bartender. She wouldn't let me quote her directly, or use her surname, as she isn't into anything remotely to do with brands, let alone a book like this.

But that's not to say that she hasn't got a decent appetite when it comes to cultural consumption; it's just that she won't buy into any mass-produced brands. She hates all coffee chains, especially Starbucks (don't even mention McDonald's or KFC). She will only shop locally – St. Mark's Bookshop, Strand Book Store, Bleecker Street Records, 4th Street Food Co-op – even if she can't really afford to. She goes to the Village East Cinema and drinks Brooklyn beer at such places as Arlene's Grocery and the Lit Lounge. She sounds like a living cliché, but Jennifer M. is Unbrandable, almost off the radar.

#53
Words with the Shaman: Frank Sinatra Jr

As I may have mentioned a couple of times already, my favourite brand in the whole wide world is Stüssy. And as this book is about truth and brands, I felt I had to include Stüssy's backstory. I have previously documented the creative and public-facing aspects of the brand, but not the internal, business side. This was the domain of the excellently named Frank Sinatra Jr (no relation), who started the company with Shawn Stüssy back in 1984. Up until Frank's involvement, Shawn had been making and selling his own surfboards, which he signed with his surname. He began adding his signature to items of clothing, and it was when he needed some money to screen-print what was now the Stüssy logo on to 200 T-shirts that Frank stepped in. The rest, as they say, is history.

I meet up with Frank in California one September morning. He's about to take his dog for a walk, so I tag along. Soon we're talking about the streetwear industry, and in particular about the well-financed organizations that have a slick-as-fuck business plan with very aggressive goals, but which only ever turn out a sequence of shite, soulless brands – what the mass-market thinks it wants. Thankfully, as Frank points out, the industry has another dimension to it. 'The other side is the natural, organic brand that starts with a particular niche vision [that] will allow it to grow a little bit without the backing of a conglomerate. But most of these people have no clue about how deep the demand will be or where it will take them, how long it will be. So when Shawn and I started out it was a very flexible ambition … Shawn only wanted to make thirty- to fifty-thousand bucks a year, and I just wanted to see this thing get off the ground so we could begin to pay ourselves a salary and we would take what came. There was no long vision. The long vision came because the immediate vision was so pure and that never changed.'

For me, one of the most interesting aspects of Stüssy is the International Stüssy Tribe (IST), a kind of brand within a brand. I ask Frank how it came about. 'We'd been making these varsity jackets,' he explains, 'and because Shawn was hanging out with [record producer] Michael Koppelman, [fashion designer] Peter 'Barnzley' Armitage and [video director and graphic artist] James Lebon, he made special jackets for them. They all had dope colour combinations, a variety of unique prototypes, all with "IST" on them but in a variety of colours. Collectable. The tribe grew out of the fact that these guys were wearing these unique jackets and it became notable that they were the core members of this inner circle.' *The Face* magazine ran a photo of the London IST, which encapsulated everything that anyone could ever want from the brand: effortlessly cool, nothing contrived, no big idea, no gimmick or fake USP. The real deal.

The conversation returns to the subject of allowing brands to grow organically. If you try and force a brand to grow too quickly, you will ultimately lose. You have to be in it for the long haul. I ask Frank for his thoughts on growing a brand like Stüssy. 'You're fighting a battle,' he observes, 'because what I've found lacking in 99 per cent of companies – large or small – is patience. Nobody has confidence that it will last, and neither are they willing to allow it to mature. There is either the pressure of the financials or the pressure of ambition, and now you can add pressure from the retail channels. These days the actual retailers push hard for you to grow fast so they can have their big hit this month or year. They want to capitalize on who you are before someone else does. And so you've got pressure from all angles to be something you're not by growing faster than you should. Patience is no longer around, and it's a very important virtue for building a long-lasting brand.'

In 1996, having decided that he wanted to spend more time with his family, Shawn left Stüssy, selling his portion of the business to Frank. The departure of a founding member of a business or brand or whatever can often spell disaster, since the vision sometimes disappears with them.

How did Stüssy cope? 'The first thing we did was that we didn't panic. I had all kinds of people writing articles asking "Can Stüssy exist without Stüssy?" Shawn was the only designer we had in the company. Shawn was it. So there was a big void to fill. But I had the luxury of some existing business with our Japanese customers, and some very good friends around the world – Michael Koppelman flew out many times, [Supreme founder] James Jebbia, [Undefeated co-founder] Eddie Cruz – we all put our heads together. But I wasn't panicking because I hadn't yet seen the complete elimination of [options]. We were being rejected very quickly in America, but we were not being rejected so quickly in Japan.'

It was by ensuring that its Japanese customers received their orders on a proper seasonal basis that Stüssy was able to start growing again. But this upturn lasted only a short while. Over to Frank: 'By 2000 we kinda fell off that initial resurgence, and we were back to the reality of returning the brand to a sense of originality and authenticity, of finding a customer that is going to be a passionate spokesman for us for a while. At the time, [everyone was into] thrift-shop crap: plaid, punk, grunge – throughout the world we were going through a really bad fashion period. Yet Stüssy didn't want to go there, and we were really counter to the massive trends that were going on and we looked out of place. Ralph Lauren looked out of place back then as classics were dying, they looked kind of boring. But just like them we said this is who we are; we're not going to change who we are to suit what today's flavour is. It was a long period of trying to find that balance between who we wanted to be and what enough people wanted us to be, to find a serious customer in volume.'

Frank struggled with the challenge of reconnecting Stüssy with its true audience – a passionate group of people who would help him rebuild the brand, bring it back to the forefront – for more than six years. He tried almost everything, from remixing the clothes to ad campaigns shot by such photographers as Jürgen Teller and Terry Richardson, but without success. 'I was open to anything', says Frank. 'A world skate-team tour, collaborations with [video skate magazine] *411* – I paid big bucks for that. I was throwing money at experiments, to see which one would get me any traction, any response. And I found that not one of them did, especially with the younger audience. It did with the intelligentsia; they would notice it, but they're not my customers – they get their clothes for free. The kids, the next generation needed to begin to accept our movement. I was really trying to find anything that had a sense of class to it to resonate with this new audience. It turned out in the end it was the whole sneaker culture, paired up with online social-media marketing and Web culture. That finally was what opened the door.'

For many years Stüssy's marketing and communications strategy had been based on two-page magazine spreads. Looking back, however, these ads were rather flat and lacked any sense of story, apart from who had shot them and who they featured. There was no substance there. They told people that Stüssy was up for experimenting and that it knew how to be creative, but they didn't feature an authentic narrative – something that Stüssy has in buckets. So when the brand started pulling together Web features and blogs and sneaker collaborations, with a story that told the true nature of the brand, Stüssy's authenticity and heritage came shining through for a new generation. 'It took a few years,' remembers Frank, 'but that's when I feel everything started back up again. Now I have a storyline that I can build on. The Internet is the only way to reach this new generation. They don't care about magazines. The old ways of reaching them are gone, and the retailers had already edged us out. They had become lifeless, homogenous stores that moved massive amounts of commoditized apparel. They were definitely not brand builders. So you're not going to reach these kids by being in cool little surf or skate shops anymore.'

Central to Stüssy's ability to connect with its core audience was the involvement of Frank's son. Including the youth in the control and development of a brand is something that I've been banging on about for years: to connect with the youth you have to work with the youth. They have to be your Mad Men. 'I have the benefit of a twenty-six-year-old son', explains Frank, 'who grew up hanging out with the Stüssy tribes around the world and touring with the skate team when he was twelve. He went from being this cool little kid to being someone with a great amount of leverage over the company because he knows how the Internet is consumed. He knows what social-media marketing should be from Stüssy's point of view. A lot of companies in the streetwear industry – not the real ones like Supreme – are run by older guys who have become a bit insular. They shelter themselves as they don't quite feel cool or comfortable anymore; they don't really know what's going on out there as it's all changed so much. As a result, they tend to let the older, established design, marketing and advertising people come up with the ideas. That route isn't fresh … But the last thing they really want to do is to work with the youth as they are hard to work with. They're not predicable. They may not deliver bang on time, nor can you even know what you're gonna get cos if the stuff is gonna to be truly spontaneous it sometimes works and it sometimes doesn't. All that stuff is a nightmare for a big company that wants a predictable, centralized media campaign.'

What, then, can be learned from Frank's story? The bottom line is don't panic. You've got to be patient, and allow a decent amount of time to rebuild and evaluate what's really going to work for your brand. You also have to think carefully about who needs to be brought into the core team – someone who has the same vision – and what effect they'll have on the overall team dynamic. Ultimately, it's about doing what you can to maintain what the brand stands for, and what you want it to become.

#54
Ten Ways to Unbrandable

'Don't try to be someone else, be yourself. No one will have the ideas you'll have. Be brave and do the things the old farts don't have the balls for. Most of my anecdotes are how I learned by getting fucked by directors or photographers just because I didn't know better. Which was good, because you learn a lot – and very fast.'

Götz Ulmer, Executive Creative Officer, Jung v. Matt

At the heart of my travels for this book – both actual and mental – was a quest to find the antithesis of the omnipotent brand, something I've spent the last few years surrounding myself with. At every turn, however, I was told that my search was futile: that brands have become way too powerful, and, more importantly, that the world's appetite for them has grown far too strong, for them to be overcome. But none of this is true. There were times when I felt like giving up; but, in the spirit of Luke Skywalker and his epic fight against the evil Galactic Empire, I never gave up hope. And this is what counts: no matter how futile it all seems, never lose sight of what you believe in. I believe that brands are capable of doing a massive amount of good, and that this far outweighs the bad that they do. This, then, is what being Unbrandable is all about.

OK, so the book didn't turn out as I'd expected (which in itself is no bad thing), mainly because when I started my research I found that way too many of the anti-branders I spoke to were unwilling to go on the record. So out of the window went the Malcolm Gladwell-esque book about quirky people living off-grid without a thought about brands. They obviously disliked brands, but they also disliked talking about it in the media (which a lot of them hated as well). But this made me examine brands in a different, more positive way, and it made this book a more personal journey into both the world of brands and the Unbrandable way of behaving. Being open and honest (about our shortcomings) is one of the first steps towards making a change.

#1
Transparency is an asset, not a risk, and every challenge is an opportunity to improve

Many brand managers/admen/PR-spinners see transparency as an enormous gamble, even though stepping up and telling the truth is the best way to begin. Start from a place of honesty and you will move forwards knowing that you are coming from a proper and honest standing. Show your hand willingly and invite the consumer to accompany you on the journey.

'You probably already knew that the Latin *ad vertere* means "to turn the mind towards". Maybe the future of advertising is more about a Socratic approach, that it's all about more sense, clarity and substance and less about "airy" promises. That it's not about pushing commercial truths in our faces (and wallets), but about respecting that we ourselves know what's best for us and simply providing good stuff. It would be a beautiful symmetry if the answer to the future of advertising were to lie in ancient history, wouldn't it? Too academic? Well, well ...'

Susanna Glenndahl Thorslund, Account Director, Forsman & Bodenfors

#2

Never stand still, as nobody really knows anything

Momentum and an open mind: two powerful factors when it comes to getting a brand off the ground. Never let anyone (especially alleged 'creatives' from the big ad agencies) tell you there is only one solution to a problem. There are many – as outlined in this book – and once a brand has started its Unbrandable quest, it is imperative to keep the momentum up. This is where the whole content industry comes into play. Brands can't keep spending huge amounts of money on TV ads (which, as I may have mentioned, don't really work), so what can a fledgling brand do to keep the story out there? Cue 'content is king' conversations. But the content, its journey and the brand have to stay true to their roots and continually move forwards.

'The supreme and continually increasing connectivity in the world has meant three things: 1) People are exposed to hundreds of thousands more stimuli than ever before, simply because it's now possible to access all sorts of information. 2) Whatever it is that interests you as a person, you'll find a global community to follow and who follows you. 3) When things change, they can change in an instant for the whole community. For advertising, this has many implications, creating both opportunities and serving up its demise, in the traditional sense. Perhaps the most important issue is that advertising and communication messaging (in general) now must be nimble, flexible and adaptable. They must be built around people – who rarely sit still. So, as advertisers, we've got to do more listening than preaching. What this ultimately means is that the role of the advertiser has now become to empower and enable people who share the same values as its brands. So its "campaigns" should be so much more than devising ads or websites or running promotions.

They should instead be about an integrated effort in designing the most useful platforms for people. Places where brands get to set the guidelines (based on an intimate understanding of the communities they choose to be involved with) and people get to steer. The role of the advertiser has thus now well and truly changed from creator to curator.'

Livio Tronchin, creative director

#3

Always ooze authentic, 'fight the power' attitude – but at the same time have a positive attitude and impeccable cultural heritage

'I don't get my authority from this pre-existing paradigm, which is quite narrow and only serves a few people. I look elsewhere for alternatives that might be of service to humanity. Alternate means, alternate political systems ... I say, here's the thing it shouldn't do: shouldn't destroy the planet, shouldn't create massive economic disparity, shouldn't ignore the needs of the people. The burden of proof is on the people with the power.'

Russell Brand, comedian and actor

Although he was talking about a political revolution – during his now infamous ding-dong with Jeremy Paxman on BBC Two's *Newsnight* programme – Mr Brand gave the world a truly Unbrandable moment. Here was an international, A-list star telling it like it is on national television (and then globally via YouTube), and for once there was someone out there really making sense, really trying to make a difference. It struck a chord with me as that's what I wanted to do with this book.

Regardless of his overall message (don't vote as a politician will get in), Mr Brand was projecting an undeniably authentic attitude; and for a very short space of time I was hooked, converted to the cult of Brand. And I'm a cynical bastard at the best of times.

Once a brand has caught the consumer's eye or ear with the right attitude, the next thing to think about is cultural heritage. First of all, how do you capture a pure cultural spirit? What's cultural and what's commercial? Tapping into the customer's cultural DNA is the only way to connect a brand with a strand of sub-, street or youth culture.

'Using rebellion to sell products is relatively easy providing you have a brave client – because it's all about challenging the status quo. And we all know that without challenging the status quo, there is no progress. Virgin have done OK being rebellious, haven't they?'

Matthew Bull, Creative Director, The Bull-White House

#4
The product must be solid with no planned obsolescence; commitment to innovation and sustainability is a must

Start at the beginning: look at the brand you are about to create. For the rest of you out there, look at how you can reinvent or re-position your brand. If you are going to start at a place of total honesty, the product cannot have any hidden costs. One way to make this idea work is to remember that collaboration enables systematic change, while design allows you to prototype the future rather than retrofit the past. If you don't know how to clear your brand conscience, find someone who does and collaborate with them. Make it a solid proposition. Think clean, stay clean, and people will notice.

'You often get a brief that says make a brand cool. Like, are you fucking kidding me? So, to make it cool, define cool – what is cool? … Cool is being authentic, idiosyncratic, being real. Be in that space; be who you are and if there's an amends to be made, make the amends. You most often don't have to apologize, just change your behaviour … just behave differently.'

Leroy Tulip

#5
The creators and the brand have to be accessible

Pay attention to the details and let the consumer know everything about the product. Make sure that the brand has the best after-sales service imaginable, then use this service to listen to your consumers: it all comes back to their narrative. This can take the form of singing praise or complaining about a defect. Nobody and nothing is perfect, so whatever the problem – big or small – the brand needs to be able to sort it out. Sounds obvious, but for a lot of brands it isn't. And remember: the consumer will get more satisfaction with more human communication and less satisfaction with less human communication.

'There are these other themes going on – this whole notion of the hive mind, crowdsourcing, lots of people doing things together … There are some views of the world, which are of course hypothetical, that say that there's an unconscious global spirit brain that we share … and that's how people come together because they connect somehow at some other level. There are things that are happening in the digital world that seem to be mimicking this … Then I wonder whether the way we live our lives, in terms of resource use – how many pairs of trainers we buy, whether we start to buy clothes that [can be worn] for five years rather than six months – all these kinds of trends are all moving to a more community view of what our race is. I think it's a mega trend that is really interesting … potentially [it] changes everything.'

Omaid Hiwaizi

#6

Brands have the power to be an independent and truthful voice in a sea of co-opted/bought media

'Yes, brands do have the power to be independent and truthful in a sea of co-opted/bought media … the question is whether they choose to express it or not. Too often, brands adopt the position of "better to say nothing than risk offending people by saying something". But that doesn't mean they have to adopt that stance, and it doesn't mean that speaking out – even if they're a massive corporation – would result in ridicule. Scepticism, yes. Ridicule, no. At least in theory.

However, there is another way of looking at it … and that is whether it's actually wrong for a brand to express a "self-interested" view. Now, many would say, "Yes, Rob, it is wrong", but is it really that simple? For me, the key is down to what they say and why they're saying it. If they're basically trying to scare/blackmail/con people into conversations or considerations … then yes, I would agree it's a terrible thing to do … but if their perspective is based on a genuine belief that runs through the heart of the company and has a real relevance to the cultural context that they wish to be a part of, then maybe not. It's a fine line, I totally get

that, but all I'm saying is that the answer isn't as clear-cut as many may like to claim.'

Rob Campbell

Brands have the power to do good, to be a catalyst for change. To that end, the role of the brand has evolved from creator to curator, and this raises questions to do with the relationship between brands and the individual. Quite a lot of what's going on in the world right now – 'big data', social media, crowdsourcing, the whole conversation about privacy – is having a massive effect on the individual. Unknown to us, it's starting to make us behave in similar ways. OK, so we all like to think that we're being so unique with our tweets and our posts and our videos and our photos, but we're not: we're all behaving in exactly the same way. The modern concept of the individual is also having a huge impact on the world's resources, as we all want to have our own identity, we all want to do our own thing. And this makes for a lot of unhappiness. So how will individuality, something that is paramount to being Unbrandable, be seen in the future – as a passing fad? Will it just be viewed as an artificial construct invented by some ancient Greek philosopher? Perhaps we'll all end up having to go back to being a sustainable, community-focused organism. These are questions that brands cannot afford to ignore.

'Even though some brands do good for the community and they give back, I don't feel they truly understand the impact they can have on a person's life. A child can feel neglected if they don't have the right brands. I can sit here and talk about what happens to the child once they've grown up, and how they can try all manner of ways to get money to buy the things they want, but is it what they really want? Or is it something they feel they must have?'

Alan Cooper

#7
Brands have to be allowed to exist within
a particular culture

There is always a short period of time before a given culture is infiltrated
by people who understand enough about it to monetize it. In that
time, the active, authentic participants of that culture create their own
'products', be it fashion, music, art or film. This has to be a consideration
when creating authentic brand content, but first the brand has to be
allowed into the culture by the gate-keepers. From the outside, brands
often appear to own a culture – we wear brands, we drive brands – but
this is not really the case. Successful brands are the ones that have been
allowed into a culture. Think Nike and sneaker-heads, Kindle and the
literati, Patagonia and mountains, Red Bull and extreme sports.

The interesting and brand-relevant cultures in this world are all
happening off-line. They're happening in trailer parks in Montagu,
Western Cape; in bedroom-based recording studios in Barnsley, South
Yorkshire; in townships in Jamaica; in tower blocks in Shanghai. Nothing
actually happens online, nothing is ever created there; rather, it's just a
place where word of these events gets reported back to you, the reader.
From front line to hyper-reality, as it were.

'Whereas the creative seeks to tap into the zeitgeist,
to mine the vast imagination and capacity for
questioning in youth, to take all that ingenuity and
idiosyncrasy and make it fit into the hegemony, the
artist is of course doing the exact opposite. Personally,
I don't like those that can find the perfect fit; I like
misfits. I hope that this parsing does not seem too
academic to you. We are both in love with the social
aspects of a certain kind of cultural production, but
we must in this always tether our fetishistic affections
to an understanding of their politics. That to me is the
simple difference between being subversive versus
acquiescent. I'm not a particularly political writer, nor

even much of an activist, but this is not to say that
these things do not matter in how we come to
see the world.'

Carlo McCormick, writer and curator

#8
**Look after your employees and your
customers will feel the benefits**

This is a no-brainer, really: just do it.

#9
**Less is more: the game changers are always
based on a simple premise**

Timing is everything. Pick your targets carefully – something locally
relevant is always good – but don't overthink it. Often, your first idea is
your best. Dig deep and consider every single thing you need to cover.
Look around and do your research properly; something will catch your
eye or heart or mind. These are not easy tasks, but nothing worthwhile
comes easily, and great work is often born of mistakes. In the commercial
world success has many fathers, while failure is an orphan. As a result, the
people who control the money are often unwilling to take risks and have
absolutely no faith in the unknown. They always want a sure thing, which
means they back the idea with the best odds – the lowest-hanging fruit.
But this attitude is all wrong. It's also brand suicide, and must be
avoided at all costs.

**'The Dunlop TV ad ["Tested for the Unexpected",
1993, a groundbreaking and experimental ad that
influenced the next generation of directors] was an
instance where the stars all came together at the right**

point. I was working with a creative team from an ad agency, and they trusted me completely. I'd just come off making a terrible British Airways commercial, which really went completely wrong, so I said to them and their client, "If you want me to do this for you then you have to back off and let me do my thing otherwise I won't be able to give you what you really want." And they all did. Originally the script was "Open on a big frying pan with a car driving round the frying pan and it's got these tyres." That was what their idea was. And we completely changed it and got something out on TV that if it ran next week, it would be as radical as it was then.'

Tony Kaye

#10
Your brand story starts with the consumer

The masses move in mysterious ways, especially when it comes to their viewing habits. All the digital content that has gathered any kind of real momentum – i.e. major viewing figures, and these days that means hundreds of millions of views – has been created outside the standard ad-agency model. That is a stone-cold fact, and so is this: the future of connecting brands with the public is about curating/inspiring user-generated stories that can then be repackaged to meet the requirements and answer the needs of the brand. The two observations in this book that are guaranteed to generate the most disdain and hostility from the advertising industry are 'the story is king' and 'content generated by the consumer is the future of brand communications', simply because they remove the power from the agencies – not to mention the massive revenues they generate from marking everything up. Nevertheless, this is the future, and, perhaps most importantly, this is the way to be Unbrandable.

'I am a photographer and an imagineer. I try to produce images that will become the historical human memory. My work has evolved with the changes in time, social conditions and politics. I try to take the right images for the right time.'

Oliviero Toscani, photographer

With regards to the future of the brand, the right story (for which read 'content') for the right time (i.e. right here, right now) must come from the consumer. It has taken me twenty-one years of working in the creative industries to reach this conclusion, to understand where it's all heading – and it's all about the brand story being believable. And for this to be possible it has to be real, not some fabulous copy or amazing editorial or great big idea. It has to be a story that people can relate to – 'That's a bit of me', etc. It has to say something to someone about his or her life.

The consumer has stopped responding to the ideas thrown out by the creatives of the advertising agencies. They want to see their own lives reflected back at them in relevant and entertaining content. The agencies will never be able to produce this kind of work as they are too obsessed with controlling everything, including the generation of ideas. The majority of ad agencies are still working within the boundaries established in the middle of the twentieth century by the American advertising executive William 'Bill' Bernbach, who moved the copywriter and art director into the same room and established the 'creative team'. It was a stroke of genius at the time, but in this day and age it is as obsolete as the dinosaurs that are somehow still running the advertising industry. Add to this the idea that infiltration is the new disruption: people are sick of having their lives interrupted. They want to be able to chose what they consume and when without interruption from anyone or anything. The brands that really make an impact with the consumer do it in a very subtle and meaningful way.

#55
The Last Word

'It's difficult to imagine because we are gradually getting used, you see, to living under conditions, which in the days of our parents – my parents or grandparents – would have been regarded as intolerable. And so what is darkness? You see, everybody thinks a catastrophe is something that happens from one day to the next – like a big earthquake or something like this. But what we are not easily getting used to is a slow-motion catastrophe such as we can see happening in large parts of Africa today.'

Eric Hobsbawm

Having worked in a number of different disciplines, I've seen all sides to everything: the rage of the downtrodden; the general public wanting more bang for their buck (i.e. choices informed by price, not product); the creative free spirits rising and wrapping themselves around everything, tying it all up in knots; the brands trying to keep up; the advertising agencies trying to control something they don't understand. But it was only when I'd bounced from Seattle to the Cape Flats to Joburg to São Paulo to Berlin to Toulouse to Jerusalem that I began to understand the difference between then and now: how the brands and all their supporting industries have changed so dramatically, and how there are many, many different strands to this globally branded culture that more often than not is these days used to peddle sneakers, soda and other digital dreams.

I move about this world scribbling notes that I turn into stories and taking photos that often end up accompanying them. Sometimes I make films, and sometimes these moments of my life come together and are published between two bits of laminated cardboard. Sometimes they're put online and people write stupid comments about them, as the culture dictates. And sometimes my knowledge is used to help brands spread their word, and deep down I know I should be truly sorry that it has come to this – that, in effect, I've been reduced to a schmutter schlepper – but at the end of the day it's all right, really. So is this what culture has become? Something to consume, something we use to divert our minds for a moment, at the slightest hint of boredom? But remember: boredom is important. It is out of boredom that original culture is born. And there is less and less boredom going down these days as no one can take it anymore. They'd rather be consuming. Let's get lost again …

Sources

All quotations are taken from interviews conducted by Adam N. Stone between 2012 and 2014, with the exception of the following:

Page 9: Kalle Lasn, taken from *Meme Wars: The Creative Destruction of Neoclassical Economics*, London, 2012, n.p.

Page 13: Edward Bernays, taken from *Propaganda* [1928], New York, 2005, p. 37

Page 16: Adam Yauch, aka MCA, taken from Alan Light, 'The Story of Yo: The Oral History of the Beastie Boys', *Spin*, September 1998, available online at www.spin.com/articles/story-yo-oral-history-beastie-boys (accessed July 2014)

Pages 16–17: Michael Diamond, aka Mike D, taken from Light, 'The Story of Yo'

Page 17: Chuck D, taken from *Beastie/ography*, MTV, 11 July 1998

Page 27: Dave Hakkens, taken from 'A Mobile Phone Made of Detachable Blocks: Phoneblock [*sic*]', *archilovers.com*, www.archilovers.com/stories/4236/a-mobile-phone-made-of-detachable-blocks-phoneblock.html (accessed July 2014)

Page 28: Edward Bernays, quoted in *The Century of the Self* (television series), dir. Adam Curtis, BBC Four, 2002

Page 29: Herbert Marcuse, taken from *One-Dimensional Man: Studies in the Ideology of Advanced Industrial Society* [1964], Boston, MA, 1991, p. 9

Page 34: Helen Landon Cass, taken from a speech delivered to a convention of salesmen in Philadelphia, as reported in the *Philadelphia Retail Analyst*, 6 June 1923

Page 35: John Pilger, taken from *The War You Don't See*, dir. Alan Lowery and John Pilger, Dartmouth Films, 2010

Pages 37–8: Banksy, taken from Keegan Hamilton, 'An Interview with Banksy, Street Art Cult Hero, International Man of Mystery', *Village Voice*, 9 October 2013, available online at www.villagevoice.com/2013-10-09/art/banksy-better-out-than-in-new-york-residency-street-art-graffiti (accessed July 2014)

Pages 48–9: Seth Lubove, taken from 'Youngest American Woman Billionaire Found with In-N-Out', *bloomberg.com*, 4 February 2013, www.bloomberg.com/news/2013-02-04/youngest-american-woman-billionaire-found-with-in-n-out.html (accessed July 2013)

Page 49: Lynsi Snyder, taken from 'Lynsi Leads In-N-Out Burger with a Strong Attachment to Her Family History', *in-n-out.com*, www.in-n-out.com/history.aspx#2010 (accessed July 2014)

Page 50: Leighsa Henderson, comment on Jessica Elgot, 'In-N-Out Burger's Hendon Pop-Up Causes London Frenzy', *huffingtonpost.co.uk*, 16 October 2012, www.huffingtonpost.co.uk/2012/10/16/in-n-out-burgers-hendon-_n_1969727.html (accessed July 2014)

Sources

Page 52: Barack Obama, taken from a presidential campaign speech, Grand Rapids, Michigan, 2 October 2008, available online at www.presidentialrhetoric.com/campaign2008/obama/10.02.08.html (accessed July 2014)

Pages 53–4: Victor Lebow, taken from 'Price Competition in 1955', *Journal of Retailing*, 31, Spring 1955, quoted in *The Story of Stuff*, dir. Louis Fox, written by Annie Leonard, Free Range Studios, 2007, http://storyofstuff.org/movies/story-of-stuff (accessed July 2014)

Page 62: Don McCullin, taken from Carole Cadwalladr, 'Don McCullin: "Photojournalism has had it. It's all gone celebrity"', *theguardian.com*, 22 December 2012, www.theguardian.com/artanddesign/2012/dec/22/don-mccullin-photojournalism-celebrity-interview (accessed July 2014)

Page 80: Lars von Trier, taken from *Side by Side*, dir. Christopher Kenneally, Company Films, 2012

Page 83: 'almost two-thirds of all American teenagers ...', taken from Amanda Lenhart *et al.*, 'Teens and Social Media', Pew Internet & American Life Project, 19 December 2007, available online at www.pewinternet.org/2007/12/19/teens-and-social-media (accessed July 2014)

Pages 111 and 111–12: Douglas Tompkins, taken from Jo Confino, 'How Technology has Stopped Evolution and Is Destroying the World', *theguardian.com*, 11 July 2013, www.theguardian.com/sustainable-business/technology-stopped-evolution-destroying-world (accessed July 2014)

Page 117: Manfred Max-Neef, taken from Lasn, *Meme Wars*, n.p.

Page 120: George Monbiot, taken from 'Smart Phones, Dumb Companies', *monbiot.com*, 11 March 2013, www.monbiot.com/2013/03/11/smart-phones-dumb-companies (accessed July 2014)

Page 121: Nokia statistics taken from J. M. Ledgard, 'Digital Africa', *Intelligent Life*, Spring 2011, available online at http://moreintelligentlife.com/content/ideas/jm-ledgard/digital-africa?page=full (accessed July 2014)

Page 128: Markus Persson, aka Notch, taken from *Minecraft: Story of Mojang*, dir. Paul Owens, 2 Player Productions, 2012

Pages 132–3: Philip Graves, taken from 'Brands Behaving Badly', *campaignlive.co.uk*, 28 March 2013, www.campaignlive.co.uk/news/1176271 (accessed July 2014)

Page 155: Adam Price, taken from interview by Raymond Buchanan, BBC Scotland, 28 February 2013, available online at www.bbc.co.uk/news/uk-scotland-21595358 (accessed July 2014)

Page 156: Alan Moore, taken from 'Alan Moore – Writer', *HARDtalk*, BBC News Channel, 10 April 2012

Page 166: Russell Brand, taken from interview with Jeremy Paxman, *Newsnight*, BBC Two, 23 October 2013

Page 175: Eric Hobsbawm, taken from interview with Michael Ignatieff, *The Late Show*, BBC Two, 24 October 1994

Further Reading and Watching

Books

Benson, Richard (ed.), *Night Fever: Club Writing in The Face, 1980–1997*, London, 1997

Bernays, Edward, *Propaganda*, New York, 1928

Bernays, Edward, *Biography of an Idea: Memoirs of Public Relations Counsel Edward L. Bernays*, New York, 1965

Della Femina, Jerry, *From Those Wonderful Folks Who Gave You Pearl Harbor: Front Line Dispatches from the Advertising War* [1971], Edinburgh, 2010

Ewen, Stuart, *PR! A Social History of Spin*, New York, 1996

Hebdige, Dick, *Subculture: The Meaning of Style*, London, 1979

Kalman, Maira and Ruth Peltason (eds), *Colors – Issues 1–13: The Tibor Kalman Years*, London, 2002

Lasn, Kalle, *Meme Wars: The Creative Destruction of Neoclassical Economics*, London, 2012

LeDuff, Charlie, *US Guys: The True and Twisted Mind of the American Man*, New York, 2006

Leonard, Annie, *The Story of Stuff: The Impact of Overconsumption on the Planet, Our Communities, and Our Health – And How We Can Make It Better*, New York, 2011

Marcus, Greil, *Lipstick Traces: A Secret History of the Twentieth Century*, Cambridge, MA, 1989

Marcuse, Herbert, *One-Dimensional Man: Studies in the Ideology of Advanced Industrial Society* [1964], Boston, MA, 1991

Morin, Edgar *et al.*, *Jean-Paul Goude* (exhib. cat.), Musées des Arts Décoratifs, Paris, 2011–12

Reynolds, Simon, *Retromania: Pop Culture's Addiction to Its Own Past*, London, 2011

Sullivan, John Jeremiah, *Pulphead: Dispatches from the Other Side of America*, London, 2012

Zinn, Howard, *The Zinn Reader*, New York, 1997

Films

Bones Brigade: An Autobiography, dir. Stacy Peralta, Nonfiction Unlimited, 2012

Burp! Pepsi v. Coke in the Ice-Cold War, dir. John Pilger, Central Independent Television, 1984

The Century of the Self (television series), dir. Adam Curtis, BBC Four, 2002

Fela Kuti: Music Is the Weapon, dir. Jean-Jacques Flori and Stéphane Tchalgadjieff, Antenne 2 – KICS/Ministère de la Culture, 1982

The Greatest Movie Ever Sold, dir. Morgan Spurlock, Snoot Entertainment/ Warrior Poets, 2011

Last Shop Standing: The Rise, Fall and Rebirth of the Independent Record Shop, dir. Pip Piper, Blue Hippo Media, 2012

Minecraft: Story of Mojang, dir. Paul Owens, 2 Player Productions, 2012

Only the Young, dir. Elizabeth Mims and Jason Tippet, Oscilloscope Laboratories, 2012

The Stuart Hall Project, dir. John Akomfrah, Smoking Dogs Films, 2013

TPB AFK: The Pirate Bay Away from Keyboard, dir. Simon Klose, Nonami *et al.*, 2013

12 O'Clock Boys, dir. Lotfy Nathan, Mission Films/Prospekt, 2013

The Unknown Known, dir. Errol Morris, History Films *et al.*, 2013

Websites

adbusters.org
beastieboys.com
beppegrillo.it
deuscustoms.com
favelapainting.com
forteprenestino.net
in-n-out.com
johnaltman.org
mojang.com
muji.com
npr.org
nudiejeans.com
patta.nl
pbs.org
phillypainting.org
thepiratebay.se
rogerballen.com
shakespeareandcompany.com
storyofstuff.org
stussy.com
tompkinsconservation.org
villagevoice.com

The Guest List

William Baglione, artist, São Paulo

Roger Ballen, photographer, Johannesburg

Banksy, artist, London

Trevor Beattie, adman, London

Hajo de Boer, cookie-baker and adman, Amsterdam

Russell Brand, comedian and actor, Los Angeles

James Brown, Mash Design, Adelaide

Jeremy Brown, founder and CEO, Sense Worldwide, London

Matthew Bull, Creative Director, The Bull-White House, New York

Rob Campbell, strategist, Shanghai

Marylin Cayrac, photographer, Toulouse

Alan Cooper, Prince's Trust Young Ambassador, Luton

BJ Cunningham, propagandist, London

Bill Drummond, musician, artist and writer, London

Martin Eberle, photographer, Berlin

Joey Elgersma, creative director, Berlin

Andrew Essex, Vice Chairman, Dro5a, New York

Denzyl Feigelson, Music Synergist, iTunes, London

DeAnna Forbes-Sanchez, teenage entrepreneur, London

Gee, co-founder, Patta, Amsterdam

Philip Graves, writer, London

Beppe Grillo, comedian, blogger and political activist, Rome

Haas & Hahn (Jeroen Koolhaas and Dre Urhahn), social artists,
    Amsterdam/Philadelphia

Dave Hakkens, founder, Phonebloks, Amsterdam

Jake Hanrahan, journalist, London

Omaid Hiwaizi, Chief Strategy Officer, Geometry Global UK, London

Tama Janowitz, writer, New York

Hugo Kaagman, artist, Amsterdam

Tony Kaye, director and ex-adman, Los Angeles

Erik Kessels, creative director, Amsterdam

Tarryn-Lee Lamb Warner, anthropologist, Port Elizabeth

Kalle Lasn, co-founder, Adbusters Media Foundation, Vancouver

Annie Leonard, sustainability champion, Berkley, California

Onno Lixenberg, cookie-baker and adman, Amsterdam

Celso Loducca, Brazilian advertising legend, São Paulo

Josie Long, comedian, London

Seth Lubove, journalist, Los Angeles

Carlo McCormick, writer and curator, New York

Don McCullin, photographer, Somerset

Rian Malan, writer, Johannesburg

Manfred Max-Neef, economist and environmentalist, Chile

George Monbiot, writer, Oxford

Alan Moore, writer, Northampton

Victoria Nyberg, strategist at Wednesday, London

Barack Obama, President of the United States, Washington DC

Markus 'Notch' Persson, founder, Mojang, Stockholm

John Pilger, journalist, writer and film-maker, London

Malcolm Poynton, Global Chief Creative Officer, Cheil, London

Adam Price, screenwriter and producer, Copenhagen

Peter Robinson, researcher and heritage-brand specialist, Leeds

Frank Sinatra Jr, entrepreneur, Irvine, California

Lynsi Snyder, President and Owner, In-N-Out Burger, Bradbury, California

Casius Stone, former gamer, Batley

Franca Silvi Taylor, Adam N. Stone's Italian *nonna*, Rome

Susanna Glenndahl Thorslund, Account Director, Forsman & Bodenfors, Gothenburg

Douglas Tompkins, environmentalist and entrepreneur, USA

Oliviero Toscani, photographer, Cecina

Lars von Trier, film-maker, Hvidovre

Livio Tronchin, creative director, Cape Town

Leroy Tulip, consumer insight specialist, Johannesburg

Götz Ulmer, Executive Creative Officer, Jung v. Matt, Hamburg

Irvine Welsh, writer, Edinburgh

Sylvia Whitman, proprietor, Shakespeare and Company, Paris

Index